*Against*
*the*
*Night*

# *Against the Night*

## LIVING IN THE NEW DARK AGES

# CHARLES COLSON
with Ellen Santilli Vaughn

SERVANT PUBLICATIONS
ANN ARBOR, MICHIGAN

Vine Books is an imprint of Servant Publications especially designed to serve evangelical Christians.

Published by Servant Publications
P.O. Box 8617
Ann Arbor, Michigan 48107

99  00  01  02  10  9  8  7  6  5  4  3  2  1

Printed in the United States of America
ISBN 1-56955-144-8

LIBRARY OF CONGRESS CATALOGING-IN-PUBLICATION DATA

Colson, Charles W.
    Against the night : living in the new dark ages / Charles Colson with Ellen Santilli Vaughn.
        p.    cm.
    Includes bibliogarphical references and index.
    ISBN 1-56955-144-8 (alk. paper)
    1. Christianity and culture.    2. Christian life—Biblical teaching.    I. Vaughn, Ellen Santilli.    II. Title.
BR115.C8C54    1999
261'.0973'09048—dc21                    99-26124
                                                                      CIP

To Dr. Carl F.H. Henry who has, from the earliest days of my Christian life, been an inspiration, mentor, teacher, and friend. Carl's brilliant mind and compassionate heart so fervently committed to Jesus Christ have been used by God over a long lifetime to profoundly shape the course of Christianity in the West.

# CONTENTS

# PREFACE

When the publisher first told me they intended to reprint *Against the Night*, I wondered if the material was dated. A lot has happened in ten years. What I here call "the new barbarism" has subsequently been given a classification, a "real" name that is analyzed and debated, criticized and defended: It's been labeled postmodernism, a relativistic worldview that claims the individual as its own god.

I went to my bookshelf, picked up the first edition of *Against the Night*, and reread the material. I quickly saw that in terms of its cultural critique, this book is as fresh today as when it was first published. It remains a very insightful look at modern culture—at the forces that are battling for predominance. This is a clear outline of a culture under siege.

Much of what is written here has come true. I think, for instance, of the portentous 1992 Supreme Court decision *Casey v. Planned Parenthood*, which firmly established abortion as a Fourteenth-Amendment-protected liberty and further defined liberty as the right of an individual to decide for himself the meaning of existence, indeed of the universe. In one breathtaking swipe of the pen, the Court shook the very foundations of our nation's ability to define the public good. This one decision alone indicated how far our culture has traveled into the dark ages I describe. For whenever there is a vacuum, it is inevitably filled by tyranny.

Much of what is written in this book, such as the train of court decisions including *Casey*, remains a serious threat. In the past decade, the percentage of Americans believing in absolute truth—that there are moral values that apply in all situations—has declined precipitously. Approximately three-quarters of the American public believe there is no such thing as truth. And if there is private immorality, it is without public consequences—or so one is led to believe from the Clinton impeachment. A free people that truly believes this will not remain free. Never has it been more important for us to fight the forces of darkness so they do not gain their foothold in our midst. And so I challenge all Christians to be beacons of light shining forth the love and the truth of Christ, to contend for Christian truth in every area of life.

And yet now, ten years after the original release of this book, I am in some ways, strange though it may sound, more optimistic in my outlook on the American scene. I was taught in law school that the most effective way to make your case is to cause your opponent to overstate his. That's what postmodernism is doing. Men and women today are realizing that, carried to its logical extreme, postmodernism creates a world in which they cannot live. For no one can survive in chaos. Postmodernism is imploding, and we see increased evidence of a growing disillusionment with its proponents' failed promises. Meanwhile, the Christian response is holding steady—a light that I believe will push back the darkness in ways that would have once surprised me. I say that, and yet I long ago learned from my own experience that we should never, never be surprised at the work of the Holy Spirit in this world, as the Spirit works in and through men and women who are committed to the Lord Jesus Christ and to his kingdom.

As the calendar turns on a new millennium—and many ask if it will bring doom—I remind my fellow believers that we are to be what the prophet Zechariah called "prisoners of hope," never giving sway to fear or despair. Nearly three hundred years ago, when "good Queen Anne" was dying and British Protestants feared for their future, Isaac Watts wrote a timeless—even millennial—hymn, in that it reminds us that "A thousand ages in [God's] sight/ Are like an evening gone." Drawing on themes of Psalm 90, which may have been written at a critical juncture in the history of Israel, upon the death of their "good King Josiah," the hymn is a prayer addressed to "Our God, our help in ages past,/ Our hope for years to come."

Yesterday, today, forever, we serve a God who is our help and our hope. And of him we claim:

Sufficient is thine arm alone,

And our defense is sure.

Charles W. Colson

March 1999

# THE SMELL OF SUNSET

All is ephemeral—fame and the famous as well.
—Marcus Aurelius Antoninus

It was 146 B.C. and the sun was setting over the great city of Carthage on the north coast of Africa. A brisk breeze blew off the Gulf of Tunis, hurling breakers against the outer harbor, as General Scipio Africanus climbed to a hillside overlooking the city. Across the sea, mountain peaks carved a jagged horizon; to the north lay the marshy plain of Utica.

Rome, the master Scipio served, had been dividing and conquering enemies like the Carthaginians for generations. Hundreds of thousands of troops and decades of war had expanded the powerful Roman Empire as far as its ambitions could reach.

Then had come the gross insult of the Second Punic War. Hannibal, the brilliant Carthaginian general, had dared to cross the Alps and assault the city of Rome itself. Rome's mighty army was pushed to the brink of defeat.

But in Scipio Africanus, Rome had found its match for Hannibal. Son of a proud military family, the great general rallied the Roman troops and attacked Carthage. Spurred on by the city's rich booty, Scipio's soldiers fought fiercely for three years while the 700,000 citizens of Carthage resisted with equal fervor. Scipio lost legions to their cunning and endurance.

In the end, however, the Roman army reduced the Carthaginians to a handful of soldiers huddled together inside the pillared temple of their god Eshmun. And with the enemy defeated, Scipio ordered his men to burn the city.

Now, as the final day of his campaign drew to a close, Scipio Africanus stood on a hillside watching Carthage burn. His face, streaked with the sweat and dirt of battle, glowed with the fire of the setting sun and the flames of the city, but no smile of triumph crossed his lips. No gleam of victory shone from his eyes.

Instead, as the Greek historian Polybius would later record, the Roman general "burst into tears, and stood long reflecting on the inevitable change which awaits cities, nations, and dynasties, one and all, as it does every one of us men."

In the fading light of that dying city, Scipio saw the end of Rome itself. Just as Rome had destroyed others, so it would one day be destroyed. Scipio Africanus, the great conqueror and extender of empires, saw the inexorable truth: no matter how mighty it may be, no nation, no empire, no culture is immortal.

*Part I*

*SUNSET*

# ONE

# INTIMATIONS OF DECLINE

The sun's rim dips; the stars rush out:
At one stride comes the dark.

—Samuel Taylor Coleridge,
*The Rime of the Ancient Mariner*

Two thousand years after Scipio Africanus's empty victory at Carthage, we, too, scan the horizon with unease. We sense that things are winding down, that somehow freedom, justice, and order are slipping away. Our great civilization may not yet lie in smoldering ruins, but the enemy is within the gates. The times seem to smell of sunset.

Encroaching darkness casts long shadows across every institution in our land. In the halls of academia, students and professors disdain the very philosophers who have shaped our civilization. At Stanford University, angry students demonstrated against the required reading of their Western civilization curriculum;

they carried placards of protest and shouted, "Hey, hey, ho, ho, Western culture's gotta go!" Why? Because Plato, Pascal, Darwin, and others share an elitist distinction: they were white males.

Stanford's faculty responded by adding minority and women writers to the reading list, thus revising history to accommodate a sort of retroactive affirmative action program. "Alas, if only Plato had been a lesbian Comanche," mused one observer.

The great houses of government host similar signs of deterioration. The closing months of the much-heralded Reagan revolution were stained by a series of scandalous revelations: from the Iran-Contra affair to a rash of indictments of trusted aides to the news that the president's schedule had been determined by a California astrologer. Even Reagan's most trusted advisor was targeted by investigators. "Meese is a pig" posters plastered the city of Washington while the attorney general clung to his Justice Department office, despite the mass exodus of lesser officials who refused to work for him.

In the end, Meese announced his resignation just two weeks before the 830-page report of an independent counsel concluded that the chief law enforcement officer of the United States "probably violated the criminal law," but that prosecution was not warranted because of "extenuating circumstances." Lady Justice stood in the grand hall of justice not only blind but paralyzed.

At the other end of Pennsylvania Avenue, Speaker of

the House Jim Wright, along with a growing number of elected officials, was under investigation for conflict of interest. And in the Capitol, the 535 members of Congress and their supporting cast of 25,000 staffers busily churned out bloated budgets and fat studies on such topics as the future of Belgian endive. Before the 1988 elections, three prominent and promising young senators announced plans for early retirement. Why? As one put it bluntly: the whole political process "stands on the brink of incoherence."

Ugly excesses characterized the 1988 presidential campaign. Streams of empty rhetoric effectively quenched any substantive discussion of the issues and fed the growing political disillusionment of the populace. Apathetic voters, disgusted by the vacuous campaign, stayed home from the polls. Nearly half of the eligible electorate didn't even bother to cast their ballots.

And where are the defenders of the faith in the midst of such disillusionment and cynicism? Religion itself has suffered a series of devastating blows, culminating in the hypocrisy of popular televangelist Jimmy Swaggart, who had built a multi-million-dollar religious empire by preaching the gospel and denouncing, with holy passion, the lascivious age in which we live. At the same time, it was discovered, Swaggart was exploring a different kind of passion in the cheap motels of Baton Rouge.

Meanwhile, decadence and despair haunt many of America's youth. Perhaps fourteen-year-old Rod

Matthews represents the most horrible extreme. Uninterested in baseball or books, Rod found one thing that did stimulate him: death. His curiosity was intensely aroused by a rental video, *Faces of Death,* a collage of film clips of people dying violently. He wanted to see death happen in real life.

So one winter day Rod lured a young friend into the woods and hammered him to death with a baseball bat. At Matthews's trial a child psychiatrist testified that the boy was not conventionally insane. He just "doesn't know right from wrong. . . . He is morally handicapped."[1]

Even sterile hospital corridors are not immune from the loss of standards of right and wrong. The *Journal of the American Medical Association* reported the case of an anonymous intern who was called to the bedside of twenty-year-old Debbie, a terminal cancer patient. The intern had never seen Debbie before and knew nothing about her beyond what he read on her chart and discerned—or thought he discerned—from her moans. "Let's get it over with," she murmured.

The intern measured twenty milligrams of morphine sulphate into a syringe—enough, he wrote later, "to do the job"—and injected it into Debbie's thin arm. Four minutes later her heart stopped beating. The doctor's only comment was, "It's over, Debbie." He had accomplished his goal: "to give her rest." And he only had to kill her to do it.

Indeed, the times smell of sunset.

Social critics see the darkness encroaching upon

every area of life: politics, education, law, medicine, the arts, even our communities, churches, and families. Paul Kennedy's best-selling *Rise and Fall of the Great Powers* talks of economic and military overextension and the inevitability of retreat for the West. Alasdair MacIntyre refers to "new dark ages" of moral decay. Aleksandr Solzhenitsyn warns of the West's debilitating "spiritual exhaustion." Malcolm Muggeridge, as always, paints it more colorfully: "Having educated himself into imbecility and polluted and drugged himself into stupefaction, [Western man] keeled over: a weary, battered, old Brontosaurus, and became extinct."[2]

In all this, of course, there is a powerful temptation to exaggerate the importance of one's own times. I have no idea whether we face the end of the West or not; history, not to mention the sovereign will of God, is more complex than we imagine. Caution is therefore in order as we attempt to trace the course of cultural decay.

But caution doesn't leave me without convictions. I believe that we do face a crisis in Western culture, and that it presents the greatest threat to civilization since the barbarians invaded Rome. I believe that today in the West, and particularly in America, the new barbarians are all around us. They are not hairy Goths and Vandals, swilling fermented brew and ravishing maidens; they are not Huns and Visigoths storming our borders or scaling our city walls. No, this time the invaders have come from within.

We have bred them in our families and trained them

in our classrooms. They inhabit our legislatures, our courts, our film studios, and our churches. Most of them are attractive and pleasant; their ideas are persuasive and subtle. Yet these men and women threaten our most cherished institutions and our very character as a people.

Who are these new barbarians? How have they so quietly and effectively invaded a nation that spends millions each year to defend itself from enemy attack? Can they be defeated?

The answers, which occupy the balance of this book, are as dismaying as the questions—and supremely challenging.

# THE BARBARIAN INVASION: TRACING THE ROOTS

There is nothing so absurd but some philosopher has said it.

—Cicero

The Romans believed their empire would last forever. Huge public buildings like the temple of Jupiter had stood from the beginning of the Republic, and the new Pantheon made even the lowliest citizen stop and stare. Marble pillars soaring straight into the blue skies above the city embodied Rome's grandeur and greatness.

Vast libraries contained, it was said, all the books in the world: the learning of the past enshrined for the future. Roads radiating from the Golden Milepost in the Forum seemed destined to remain arteries of the thriving life of Roman civilization for ages to come, just as they had for centuries past.

No one could remember when Rome had not been the pinnacle of civilization. Its permanence seemed as certain as its greatness.

For the people themselves, life was not only secure but pleasant. Their basic needs met, they were free to pursue every conceivable form of pleasure; and in that pursuit, the comfortable Romans were deaf to the barbarian rumblings from the East. Even as the sparks of Rome's defeat were struck within the city by its own citizens, the invasions that would fan them to full flame were already beginning far away.

I don't propose to draw precise parallels between the fall of Rome and the decline of our own civilization, but I believe we face a similar peril. The seeds of our own barbarian invasion, however, have been sown in far different soil than that which yielded Rome's destruction. Ours began in a seemingly harmless way. Profound social changes often trace their origins not to sinister conspiracies but to the paneled libraries of genial philosophers or the study alcoves of the British Museum or the crowded cafes of the universities. Powerful movements are rooted in the realm of ideas. And in this instance, I believe, we can trace the roots of modern barbarianism back to a winter day early in the seventeenth century.

It was cold and raw that day in 1610 when a French mathematician named Rene Descartes pulled his cloak around him and climbed into the side compartment of a large stove. Descartes had been wrestling for weeks with questions of doubt and reason in his search for some certainty of a philosophic system. As he warmed himself in his stove, his imagination began glowing with the light of reason, and he resolved to doubt everything that could possibly be doubted.

Hours later Descartes emerged, having determined that there was only one thing he could not doubt, and that was the fact that he doubted. A good day's work. Descartes drew the conclusion, *Cogito, ergo sum*: "I think, therefore I am." Then he went out for a cognac.

Descartes's now-famous postulate led to a whole new premise for philosophic thought: man, rather than God, became the fixed point around which everything else revolved; human reason became the foundation upon which a structure of knowledge could be built; and doubt became the highest intellectual virtue.

This triad of man, philosophical reasoning, and doubt led to the Enlightenment, an era that spawned a host of philosophic systems and intellectual movements. Different as they were, however, Enlightenment thinkers shared principles that still shape the modern mind: a new confidence in the power of human reason; a corresponding distrust of tradition; and a new freedom. Men and women could now order their lives according to what they could see for themselves through reason, and the fetters of faith and tradition fell away. For the first time the enlightened mind, explains Eric Voegelin, "could sincerely believe that it need not bother about some 1500 years of Christian history and several centuries of Hellenism."[1]

The consequences of this new freedom were far-ranging in art, literature, and, most importantly, ethics and morality. And the results were far-reaching, for they shape the modern mind.

For centuries, people had established their moral standards according to the discerned will of God or by appealing to Aristotelian concepts of virtue. Now Enlightenment thinkers sought to root morality not within a transcendent authority or classical conceptions of virtue, but within the mind and heart of man. Moral judgments would be measured by what men and women could know or feel for themselves. From this emerged the "idea of an autonomous ethics, without religious or metaphysical foundation."[2]

Establishing a moral system based solely on human reason is no easy task. But eighteenth and nineteenth century philosophers rose to the challenge. The efforts of two men, John Stuart Mill and Jean Jacques Rousseau, are particularly important to our examination of today's barbarians.

John Stuart Mill (1806-1873) created a code of morality based on self-interest. He believed that only individuals and their particular interests were important, and those interests could be determined by whatever maximized their pleasure and minimized their pain. Thus, the goal of society was to give the greatest pleasure to the greatest number of citizens.

The English philosopher had little use for history or tradition; Mill believed each generation had the intellectual capability to find answers for itself. "The only freedom which deserves the name is that of pursuing our own good in our own way," he said.[3] In his famous essay *On Liberty*, Mill went so far as to urge "eccentricity" as a life-style. "The mere example of nonconformity, the mere refusal to bend the knee to custom, is itself a service."[4]

For our purposes in this book, I will call Mill's philosophy *utilitarian individualism*, a system whereby individuals make moral judgments by rationally calculating what will multiply their pleasures and diminish any pain.

Another strain of Enlightenment influence dismissed such a sterile and calculating emphasis on rationality and rooted moral judgments in "feeling." The most celebrated champion of this *experiential individualism* was Jean Jacques Rousseau (1712-1778), the father of French romanticism. In his *Discourse on Inequality*, Rousseau argued that man's problem was civilization, not his own nature. Societal constraints on personal conduct actually generated the immorality they were intended to prevent. When men and women were left unfettered, Rousseau argued, their natural virtues were cultivated by "the voice of nature." Human passions superseded any consideration of God or reason.

Rousseau, like Mill, expressed a taste for individualistic self-expression liberated from traditional restraints. He wrote in his autobiography with a kind of exhilarated egoism, "I am different from all men I have seen. If I am not better, at least I am different." To him, man was good; experience was good; individuality was good.[5]

John Stuart Mill could not possibly have imagined

how his invitation to moral nonconformity would be embraced two centuries later by the 1960s students who burned their draft cards and defied "the establishment" with easy sex and hard drugs; or by the 1970s couples who bore children while defying the "custom" of marriage; or by the gay activists of the 1980s who flaunted their homosexuality in an attempt to destigmatize the deviant.

Nor could Jean Jacques Rousseau have envisioned the shallow adaptations of his ideas by today's experiential individualists, the New Agers, for whom self is exalted as the god within. "I am God!" shouted Shirley MacLaine in her television special about her spiritual journey. Bubbling over with vivid in-and-out-of-body experiences, Ms. MacLaine is today's supreme experientialist (though she has some utilitarian tendencies as well, since she charges several hundred dollars per seminar to teach others how to be god too).

Rousseau and Mill, in some ways, could not have been more different. One championed feeling, the other rational calculation—rather like comparing a painter and an economist. Yet they shared the one principal trait of modern thought: moral pride. Rousseau exhibited the pride of the man of passion; Mill, the pride of the man of reason. And they were united by an individualism that put man, uninhibited by tradition or anything else, at the center of the universe.

Few today read Rousseau or Mill or even know their names. Yet pale reflections of their experiential and utilitarian individualism have filtered down to form a set of moral presuppositions in our Western consciousness which have shaped many individuals in our modern world.

In 1979 sociologist Robert Bellah set out to conduct extensive interviews with two hundred average, middle-class Americans. As Bellah studied what "habits of the heart" defined the thoughts and lives of these individuals, a pattern emerged. Many had no sense of community or social obligation. They saw the world as a fragmented place of choice and freedom that yielded little meaning or comfort. They even seemed to have lost the language to express any kind of commitment to anything—church, family, community— other than themselves.

Bellah calls this "ontological individualism," by which he means the belief that the individual is the only source of meaning. He then divides ontological individualists into two categories: expressive individualists and utilitarian individualists.

Utilitarian individualists seek meaning through the calculated pursuit of material interests. For them, life is an endless quest for personal success. Expressive individualists, on the other hand, luxuriate in vivid personal feelings, seeking a life rich in experiences and relationships. While expressive individuals and utilitarian individuals may disagree about details, they have accepted the same basic orientation, dating back to Mill and Rousseau: *Me.*

Both brands of individualism stand in stark contrast to what Bellah calls "biblical" and "republican" traditions, which provide a reference point of meaning outside the individual to tell us about the nature of the world, society, and ourselves. These traditions are embodied in what Bellah calls "communities of memory" such as religious groups, traditional families, and cultural associations that communicate a sense of order and context.

Such communities of memory are in decline, Bellah asserts, since today's pervasive individualism is destroying the subtle ties that bind people together. This, in turn, is threatening the very stability of our social order as it strips away any sense of individual responsibility for the common good.

"Common good," "social order," and "cultural associations" sound like clinical terms used by social scientists locked away from the rigors and relationships of real life. But nothing could be closer to our daily lives than the conclusions of Bellah's study. For when people care only about themselves, they are not easily motivated to care about their neighbors. When relationships are based on mutual gain and people elevate their own needs above the needs of others, community life devolves into the survival of the fittest. The weak become prey for the strong. And in the end, rank individualism destroys even the best of societies.

Consider just a snapshot of this truth. In 1978, during President Carter's attempt to reinstate draft registration, newspapers across the country carried a photo that I have carried in my mind ever since: a young Princeton student defiantly wielding a poster emblazoned with the words, "Nothing is worth dying for."

To many this seemed a noble celebration of life. But if nothing is worth dying for, is anything worth living for?

While such new barbarians who know no higher law than self-interest, who see nothing to champion beyond their individualism, are celebrating their own nihilism, they are, in effect, torching the very props of virtue on which our societal experiment—and our very existence—depend. And in these flames we may well see what Scipio Africanus saw in the fires of Carthage.

Yes, the times do smell of sunset.

# THREE

# ISLANDS IN THE STREAM

I find television very educating. Every time somebody turns on the set I go into the other room and read a book.

—Groucho Marx

But wait a minute. Individualism is as American as the Fourth of July. After all, we are a nation hacked out of the wilderness by rugged individualists, a land made great by rags-to-riches immigrants who pulled themselves up to the American dream by their own bootstraps. We've been fed heroes like Daniel Boone, Paul Bunyan, and Horatio Alger with our Wheaties, while in the background Frank Sinatra croons our national theme song: "I Did It My Way."

Why, then, cast individualism as the villain of our age? The answer is that there is nothing wrong with being individuals; the problem is with the "ism." As a rule, "isms" convert healthy ideas into ideologies. Authority, for example, is a biblical notion; authoritarianism twists that good into a lust for power and repressive control. Community is good; communism is an insidious ideology. Recognition of the individual affirms respect for human dignity and the uniqueness of each person; individualism distorts that joy of identity into an ego cult of one.

This elevation and isolation of the self is not new to American life. When French statesman Alexis de Tocqueville, known for his studies of the nature and operation of democracy, wrote of his visit to the United States in the 1830s, he celebrated many of our nation's character traits. But he also saw the concomitant danger of rampant individualism, describing with alarm the prospect of every person "thrown back on himself alone, and [the] danger that he may be shut up in the solitude of his own heart."[1]

Through the years, Americans have loved or hated a long line of individualists. Poet Walt Whitman was a celebrated expressive individualist, imparting his philosophy in such poems as "Song of Myself." Gore Vidal or Truman Capote or, pardon the example, Morton Downey, Jr. might serve as more modern examples. And America's utilitarian individualists range from Ben Franklin to Henry Ford to Donald Trump.

No, individualism is not new, nor is it all bad. What is new is the dominant influence it is exerting on American life as the barriers that traditionally held it in check have all but collapsed.

During most of our nation's existence, families, neighborhoods, churches, and civic groups have served as fire walls to restrain individualism from flaming out of control. Involvement in such communities of memory—to borrow Bellah's phrase again—drew people out of themselves and encouraged their concern for the common good. These communities also provided a foundation of authority and understanding. People could discuss moral considerations and understand one another because they drew from a shared perspective of transcendent right and wrong, a standard of authority *outside* of the individual.

This changed dramatically in the 1960s when the fire wall crumbled. Sources of authority were tried and found wanting. The youth culture adopted "a visceral sense that all forms of established authority, all rules, all demands for obedience, were inherently illegitimate."[2] Individualism spread quickly among the dry tinder of spiritual emptiness in America's youth.

Having rejected the traditional institutions of family, church, and government, hippies and yippies tried to satisfy their instinctive yearning for community by organizing communes around such disorganized norms as "do your own thing," "make love, not war," "tune in, turn on, and drop out." Ironically, most of these radical individualists were merely clones of one another. And as long as the drug supply held up and they didn't overdose, they were happy clones.

Writers like Samuel Beckett, Albert Camus, and Jean-Paul Sartre became enormously popular on college campuses. Their bleak, despairing works of drama and fiction touched a chord in those who, in their search for meaning, heard only the sounds of silence. God was either dead or deaf, unable to address the meaningless, chaotic human condition; it was up to man to assert his own meaning through his own actions. In this setting the individual became the star of his own play, acting out his own script—even if the other characters failed to show up.

Perhaps nothing evokes this pessimistic view of man's condition more clearly than Samuel Beckett's play, *Waiting for Godot,* first produced in the early 1950s but now enjoying a popular New York revival. In this absurdist drama, two tramps bicker and quibble inanely about their boots, turnips, and whether to hang themselves; meanwhile they are occupied with waiting beside a spindly tree for Godot, a god-figure. Godot never arrives, but sends his boy at the end of each act to announce that he will come "tomorrow."

"What does he do, Mr. Godot?" Vladimir, one of the tramps, asks the boy at the play's end. There is silence. "Do you hear me?" Vladimir repeats. "Yes, Sir," replies the boy. "Well?" presses Vladimir. "He does nothing, Sir," the boy responds. Again, there is silence.[3]

*Waiting for Godot* brought overnight fame to Beckett. The *New York Post* heralded the play as "grotesquely beautiful and utterly absorbing." The *London Times* called it "one of the most noble and moving plays of our generation, a threnody of hope deceived and deferred but never extinguished; a play suffused with tenderness for the whole human perplexity; with phrases that come like a sharp stab of beauty and pain."[4]

This seems hyperbolic praise for a play that the less enlightened among us might be tempted to call just plain ugly and depressing. But let us try to look with the eyes of the *Times'* reviewer: the play's "tenderness," it seems, is found in the relationship of the two pitiful main characters; though they bicker and threaten to leave one another, they do stay together. And perhaps its "hope" lies in their continuing to hold on to the expectation that Godot *will* come.

John-Paul Sartre's works, which were enormously influential in the 1960s, focused on less "noble" themes. He wrote of the great freedom found in human isolation, penning the tart phrase, "Hell is other people."

Sartre believed that in every decision a person stands alone. Because there are no moral absolutes, there are no value-associated reasons to make one decision over another. We may as readily choose to ignore a neighbor rather than help him, to cheat rather than be honest, to kill rather than let live. According to Sartre, the outcome of our choices carries no moral weight. What matters is the action of choosing an outcome. And in that choice, modern men and women are solely, individually responsible; they are the authors of their own lives and masters of their own fates.

It took two centuries for the ideas planted in the Age of Reason to come to full flower in American culture; but when these beliefs concerning man's autonomy did blossom, the harvest was abundant. The expressive "do your own thing" of the 1960s evolved into the utilitarian "I'll get mine" of the 1980s. Yippies became yuppies and climbed out of communes and up the corporate ladder. Twenty years after they disrupted the 1968 Democratic Convention, former radicals and protestors were running for office, marketing barbecue cookbooks, and conducting expensive executive workshops.

It's significant to note how television, the most popular mass medium of our day, reflects and reinforces individualism. Through brief, loosely connected sensations that play on temporary but vivid emotion, television thoroughly engages an audience of one, making personal relationships unnecessary. Flick your remote control from soap opera to game show to situation comedy to political commercial and the package is the same: brightly wrapped, emotive, and dramatic. Vanna White blurs into Mary Hart into Bob Hope into George Bush. Characters like Pee-wee Herman, Dr. Ruth (who has never met a body part she didn't like), and Alf the alien become household words. Only the background music changes.

Hooking its viewers with self-satisfying sensations, television became the perfect technological partner for the 1960s experiential individualism. And when individualism's focus shifted to utilitarianism, television was again a ready mate, massaging viewers' wants and needs with its relentless promotion of acquisitiveness through advertising. "Don't you really think you deserve a Buick?" Television manipulates our emotions and our wallets with equal skill.

Long before the advent of television, long before Johnny Carson and David Letterman, philosopher Soren Kierkegaard wrote: "Suppose someone invented an instrument, a convenient little talking tube which, say, could be heard over the whole land ... I wonder if the police would not forbid it, fearing that the whole country would become mentally deranged if it were used."[5]

The talking tube may not have left the nation totally deranged, but it has surely helped loosen our moral moorings.

Today's radical individualism, which tends in most people to be a mixture of the expressive and utilitarian, has changed our public ethos. No longer are we guided by virtue or tradition. Selfish passions breed freely, unrestrained by communities of memory. Since any absolutes are an impediment to self-realization, man's "noble" goals are freedom, choice, and tolerance. Gone are any notions of duty to our fellow man and to the Creator. As a result, there is no straight edge of truth by which one can measure one's life. Truth is pliable and relative; it can take whatever shape we want. Indeed, many simply look within to find it.

I'm reminded of the New York woman who without warning left her husband and children. Some time later she surfaced in Hawaii where she was working at a store that sold hand-dipped chocolates. When asked why, she explained that she was sorry to cause her family pain, but she had finally realized she had to "find herself." This was her way of doing it. As far as I know, she's still peddling chocolates under the palms.

# THE REIGN OF RELATIVISM

Like men with sore eyes: they find the light painful, while the darkness, which permits them to see nothing, is restful and agreeable.
—Dio Chrysostom, A.D. 40-120, 11th Discourse

The example of the woman who abandoned her family to find herself in chocolate creation is both tragic and silly. But the terrible logic of individualism says that what the woman did was right: as long as she was "true to herself," she was right to leave her family behind. For if the self is the locus of truth, what more moral quest could there be than to find oneself? There is no universal truth, no absolute code of conduct; there is only truth for me and truth for you.

When enough people hold to it, this line of reasoning produces dramatic results in a nation's public values, which are the realm of ideas and assumptions by which a culture conducts itself.

During a meeting of college educators at Harvard University in the autumn of 1987, President Frank Rhodes of Cornell University addressed the issue of educational reforms, suggesting it was time for universities to pay "real and sustained attention to students' intellectual and moral well-being."

Immediately there were gasps from the audience. One angry student stood and demanded indignantly, "*Who* is going to do the instructing? *Whose* morality are we going to follow?" The audience applauded thunderously, affirming that the heckler had settled the issue by posing an unanswerable question. President Rhodes sat down, unable or unwilling to respond.[1]

In an earlier time, the obvious answer would have been to point to 2,300 years of accumulated moral wisdom, or to a rationally defensible natural law, or to the moral law revealed by God in the Judeo-Christian Scriptures. Today, however, few educators—or any other leaders who shape public attitudes—have the audacity to challenge the prevailing assumption that there is no morally binding objective source of authority or truth above the individual.

This is not the result of some sinister secular humanist conspiracy hatched in the basement of CBS. Our society, in the name of tolerance, has chosen this view. Remember the bad old days, it is argued, when people believed in absolutes and burned one another at the stake? Enlightened men and women avoid such excesses by recognizing no absolutes at all—except perhaps the absolute of blind tolerance.

Ironically, this kind of tolerance itself leads to increasing intolerance. During NBC's coverage of the Supreme Court decision striking down Louisiana's "creation science" law, news anchor Tom Brokaw interviewed the lawyer representing Louisiana. This attorney argued quite persuasively that the legislature was merely seeking to assure equal discussion of equally valid theories regarding the origins of man. Academic freedom demanded no less, he said.

Brokaw appeared frustrated and finally growled, "But weren't many sponsors of this bill *religious people*—doing this for *religious* reasons?"

Apparently, according to Brokaw's response, a person with religious motivations has no business being involved in public debate; religious convictions might contaminate public policy. Never mind that the sponsors of the legislation were explicitly seeking academic balance rather than imposing an agenda for their religious views.[2]

After I wrote about this incident in *Christianity Today,* a Texas pastor sent Tom Brokaw my column. He responded, still blissfully missing the point: "As I'm sure Mr. Colson knows, my question (which, incidentally, was not growled) was an attempt to demonstrate that the sponsors of this legislation were specifically attempting to impose their religious values on all the school children of Louisiana. That is a corruption of the Constitution."

I later wrote to Brokaw and explained that, by his reasoning, the arguments of a devout Christian politician against murder would be assumed to be an attempt to impose his or her religious values, based on one of the Ten Commandments, on all citizens. Would that also automatically be disqualified as a "corruption of the Constitution"? Brokaw never answered my letter.

Now, Tom Brokaw is not sitting in his New York office either growling—I'll concede that—or plotting the overthrow of Western civilization and the expulsion of Christians from the United States. He is an educated, professional newscaster, urbane and fairly dispassionate in his reporting. But that demeanor is precisely the point.

As C.S. Lewis wrote, "The greatest evil is not done in those sordid 'dens of crime' that Dickens loved to paint ...it is conceived and ...moved, seconded, carried, and minuted . . . in clean, carpeted, warmed, and well-lighted offices, by quiet men with white collars and cut fingernails and smooth-shaven cheeks who do not need to raise their voices."[3]

Today's barbarians are ladies and gentlemen. Yet behind their pleasant, civilized veneer lurks an unpleasant intolerance that threatens the very processes of pluralism and freedom they claim to defend.

My point is not to argue the merits of the Louisiana case, but to demonstrate something important about the prevailing secular views that moral and religious absolutists have no right to advocate their views in our relativistic public square. Brokaw's attitude, shared by many otherwise sensible people, demands that everyone has a right to express his or her own views—as long as those views do not contain any suggestion of absolutes that would compete with the prevailing standard of relativism.

This intolerance, of course, is not limited to "religious" issues. It occurs whenever secularists assume, as they almost invariably do, that the motives of religious people are always suspect and that, therefore, their views on any matter must be disqualified.

A socialist would not be disqualified from expressing views on economic issues or on the morality of feeding the poor. A Nazi would not be excluded from political debate, nor would a sadomasochist, a pedophile, a spiritualist, or an harmonic convergence convert. Their right to free expression would be vigorously defended by the same cultural elite who are so often offended when Christians express their views.

But this paradoxical intolerance produces an even deeper consequence, for it completely transforms the nature of debate, public discussion, and consensus in society. Without root in some transcendent standard, ethical judgments become merely expressions of feeling or preference. "Murder is wrong" must be translated "I hate murder" or "I prefer that you not murder." Thus, moral claims are reduced to the level of opinion.

In this context, there is no hope of eventual solution in disagreements about, say, euthanasia or pornography. Neither side's views can be right or wrong because both are merely subjective expressions of personal feeling, and there is no objective standard by which to choose one feeling over another. So both sides simply shout louder.

Take the matter of abortion. On one side of the chasm are those who advocate abortion as a fundamental human right. On the other side are those who assert that abortion is a moral evil. In a relativistic society sanitized of any objective standards of right and wrong, however, the two sides are doing nothing more than expressing feelings. There is no rational way to choose between them. Opponents grow further and further apart, differing on a level so fundamental that they are unable to even communicate. As columnist Pat Buchanan has noted, "Americans of left and right no longer share the same religion, the same values, the same codes of morality; we only inhabit the same piece of land."

When moral judgments are based on feelings alone, compromise becomes impossible. Politics can no longer be based on consensus, for consensus presupposes that competing moral claims can be evaluated according to some common standard. Politics is transformed into "civil war carried on by other means."[4] In the end, a relativism whose initial goal was tolerance yields an environment of unending moral conflict and intolerance.

In an attempt to settle increasingly bitter disagreements, our public life becomes characterized by a kind of libertarianism by default. Absolute values are off-limits when it comes to the formation of public policy.

Everyone must be allowed to pursue his or her own private good so long as some semblance of order is maintained. John Stuart Mill would be proud.

Proponents of a public square sanitized of moral judgments purport that it assures neutrality among contending moral factions and guarantees certain basic civil rights. This sounds enlightened and eminently fair. In reality, however, it assures victory for one side of the debate.

For example, if one person believes that infanticide should be illegal and another contends it should be an option, it is no compromise when government, with supposed moral neutrality, leaves the decision to private individuals. It is unconditional defeat for those opposed to infanticide: Children die.

Historically, moral restraints deeply ingrained in the public consciousness provided the protective shield for individual rights and liberties. But in today's environment of relativistic neutrality and nearly unlimited private choices, that shield can be easily penetrated. Whenever some previously unthinkable innovation is both technically possible and desirable to some segment of the population, it can be adopted.

The process by which the once unthinkable becomes acceptable is simple enough. It works like this: Some practice so offensive that it can scarcely be discussed in public is advocated by a respected expert in a respected forum. At first the public is shocked, then outraged. The very fact that such a thing could be publicly debated becomes the subject of debate. In the process, sheer repetition of the shocking gradually dulls its effect. No longer outraged, people begin to argue for positions to moderate the extreme; or they accept the premise, challenging instead the means to achieve it.

Earlier I mentioned the case of Debbie, a young woman dying of cancer. Faced with Debbie's pain as well as her certain death, a young intern injected her with enough morphine to kill her quickly.

The world was informed of Debbie's shocking story by the intern himself, who wrote up the case anonymously, but without apology, in the *Journal of the American Medical Association,* perhaps the most respected medical journal in the world.

Following publication of the article, reaction came fast and furious. Some experts dismissed the incident as fictional. Others believed it, but focused their criticism on the young doctor's lack of familiarity with Debbie's medical history.

The article's greatest effect, however, was to yank euthanasia into the public forum, where the debate centered not on the killing but on the intern's failure to check more carefully into the case.

I don't intend to be an alarmist. Legal euthanasia is still more a threat than a reality in this country. But twenty years ago who would have thought abortion would one day be a constitutional right, or that infanticide would be given legal protection? When what was once a crime becomes a debate, that debate usually ushers the act into common practice. History has proven it.

In *The Thanatos Syndrome,* novelist Walker Percy offers

a dark vision of where such compromising debates might lead us. He sets his story in the 1990s, when Qualitarian Life Centers have sprung up across the country after the landmark case of *Doe v. Dade* has "decreed, with solid scientific evidence, that the human infant does not achieve personhood until 18 months." At these centers one can conveniently dispose of unwanted young and old alike.

An old priest, Father Smith, confronts the narrator, a psychiatrist, in the following exchange.

"You are an able psychiatrist, on the whole a decent, generous, humanitarian person in the abstract sense of the word. You know what is going to happen to you?"

"What?"

"You are a member of the first generation of doctors in the history of medicine to turn their backs on the oath of Hippocrates and kill millions of old useless people, unborn children, born malformed children, for the good of mankind—and to do so without a single murmur from one of you. Not a single letter of protest in the august *New England Journal of Medicine.* And do you know what you're going to end up doing? . . ."

"No," I say. . . .

The priest aims the azimuth at me, but then appears to lose his train of thought. . . .

"What is going to happen to me, Father," I ask before he gets away altogether.

"Oh," he says absently, appearing to be thinking of something else, "you're going to end up killing Jews."[5]

Walker Percy's vision is too dark, some say. But processes initiated subtly by the new barbarians in government and the medical profession, abetted by unthinking citizens, have already allowed inhumanities on a scale unimaginable only thirty years ago—when, ironically, we were recovering from a war against, among other things, just such atrocities in Germany.

Many would argue that public values in the West have been sliding into oblivion for a long time. Relativism has relegated righteousness to the prayer closet rather than allowing it in the marketplace of public values. Yet for many years it was the very caliber of individual character in our culture that kept our societal structures strong in spite of the decline of public values. Today, it is individual character that faces relativism's most deadly attacks.

*Part II*

# NIGHTFALL

# FIVE

# DECADENCE AND DECLINE

But the fight for our planet, physical and spiritual, a fight of cosmic proportions, is not a vague matter of the future; it has already started. The forces of Evil have begun their decisive offensive. You can feel their pressure, yet your screens and publications are full of prescribed smiles and raised glasses. What is the joy about?

—Aleksandr Solzhenitsyn

I opened this book with a reference to Scipio Africanus, the great Roman general who wept bitter tears at the fall of Carthage when he foresaw in that city's flames the end of Rome itself. He was right.

By the fourth century, Huns, Vandals, and other Germanic tribes were fighting among themselves for land throughout Europe, all the while eyeing the wealth and splendor of the Roman world. Meanwhile

Rome itself had for years absorbed a steady stream of barbarians. At first, as prisoners of war they had served as slaves; later they became free peasants, and finally mercenary soldiers and even officers.

Rome was already weakened by internal political power struggles among its leaders and indolence among its citizens. Thousands had lived on the dole for years, subsisting complacently on public assistance and free public amusements such as gladiator combat and chariot races. All this combined with the assimilation of barbarians inside the empire's borders gradually diluted the traditional Roman character that had put such a premium on organization, discipline, and obedience.

With the loss of these attributes, restraints on the passions fell away. Rome's leaders competed in ever-escalating excesses of decadence—buying, bedding, and killing both humans and animals with unrestrained cruelty and concupiscence. Following their leaders, the citizens soon sank into cheaper versions of the same decadence, sating themselves on the bloodletting at the Colosseum, where men and beasts were forced to fight to the death.

Social critic Russell Kirk has defined decadence as the loss of an aim or object in life. "Men and women become decadent when they forget or deny the objects of life, and so fritter away their years in trifles or debauchery."[1]

Today's trifles and debaucheries are less horrific only because the blood flows more vicariously—from television and movie screens. That may well be the only difference. Decadent Americans, lacking an object in life beyond self, have exhausted themselves in the mistaken notion that multiplying pleasures produces happiness. Summing up the 1980s, *Newsweek* reported, "Fun became a serious business in the '80s, pursued with a grim vigor. The '80s ideal of recreation was to have MORE fun in LESS time and be DONE WITH IT."

Citing the popular novel and film *Bright Lights, Big City*, which details a yuppie's endless journey through the bars and hotels of Manhattan in pursuit of pleasure, *Newsweek* observed, "The fact that he never seemed to actually enjoy himself when he was out having fun elucidated a peculiarly '80s notion: that the pursuit of good times could be a joyless function."

Today's hedonists are creatures of evolution: polyestered discomaniacs became yuppies snorting cocaine in the bathrooms of brass-and-fern eateries, then evolved into leotard-clad health freaks sipping Perrier at the helm of computerized exercycles, who then slumped into today's couch potatoes, ordering pizza delivered with a rental movie. Home has become the new womb for those without communities; it is a place of self-nurture and escape from AIDS and other perils of modern life. Propped in front of the VCR, this self-indulgent species enjoys life without its inconveniences.

Rather than endure the hassles of child-rearing, today's couch couples can commune with *Video Baby*. For only $19.95 they get thirteen minutes with the adorable toddler on the screen. They can name her, watch her walk and coo and grin, and take her out of the VCR before she ever needs a diaper change. For those who need emotional bonding but find a child too challenging, there are *Video Dog* and *Video Cat.*

Harmless as all this sounds, the endless, objectless pursuit of pleasure inevitably ends in despair. To be governed by nothing more than the free exercise of one's passions can be the most terrifying repression of all. Like the young woman profiled some years ago in *Psychology Today* who told her psychiatrist that she was exhausted by her life-style—an endless round of parties, drugs, sex, and alcohol. "Why don't you stop?" he asked. Astonished, she sat up abruptly. "You mean I don't have to do what I want to do?"

"They are ungoverned yet unfree," said Walter Lippmann of such morally bereft and helpless souls. One of the most influential and statesmanlike American journalists of this century, acute observer of the domestic scene, Lippmann continued, "They are creatures of the passing moment who are vaguely unhappy in a boring and senseless existence. . . . The sap of life does not reach them, their tap roots having been cut."[2]

Tragically, the loss of individual character and self-restraint leads not only to personal decadence but to corporate havoc. It undermines the foundation of the social experiment that supports us all. One of the clearest and saddest examples of this is a young Marine sergeant named Clayton Lonetree.

Clayton Lonetree was lonely in Moscow. The weather was dreary, the Marine barracks were dirty, old, and cold, and he didn't get much mail. Though guard duty at the U.S. embassy was a trusted position of honor, his work was often dull and exhausting; it was a ceremonial job with little action. In letters home he doodled U.S. planes dropping bombs on Red Square; he tried writing to an old girlfriend, only to learn she had married someone else.

It was when Clayton met Violetta in the fall of 1985 that life in Moscow began to brighten. Tall, fair-skinned, and beautiful, she was a translator at the embassy. Though Clayton had been warned about fraternizing with Soviets, he had seen enough friends and superiors date Russian women to feel comfortable doing the same. He and Violetta took long walks in the park, had tea, and even managed to be alone a few times in her apartment.

Violetta introduced Clayton to her "Uncle Sasha," who peppered him with questions about his life in the United States, his political views, life in Moscow, and life in the embassy. Clayton enjoyed the older man's interest. Then one day Sasha pulled a prepared list of detailed questions from his pocket—and Clayton finally realized that Violetta's "uncle" worked for the KGB.

But Clayton kept meeting with Violetta, and with Sasha. He began making excuses to his superiors, using elaborate techniques to make sure he wasn't being followed when he met with his Russian friends. Life became more interesting—more like the spy novels Clayton loved to read.

After he had been seeing Violetta for six months, Clayton's Moscow tour came to a close. He asked to be reassigned to guard duty at the U.S. embassy in Vienna. . . .

Clayton Lonetree was lonely in Vienna. But soon Uncle Sasha arrived, bearing photographs and a letter from Violetta. As he watched the young Marine excitedly rip open the package, Sasha knew Clayton was ready for something more than talk.

The first item Clayton delivered to the KGB agent was an old embassy phone book. Next came a map of the embassy interior, for which Clayton received $1,800. He used $1,000 of it to buy Violetta a handmade Viennese gown. Then came three photographs of embassy employees thought to be CIA agents, and another $1,800 payment.

Sasha proposed an undercover trip back to Moscow, where Clayton could at last visit Violetta—and receive KGB training. Clayton arranged for vacation leave from the embassy.

But now he began to get nervous. He started to drink more; he lay awake nights trying to think of a way out of the KGB web. He hadn't realized that when he traded the trust of his nation for sex and cash, he traded his soul as well.

So in December 1986, Clayton tried to trade it back. At a Christmas party he approached the Vienna CIA chief, a man whose real identity he would not have known except that Uncle Sasha had pointed him out earlier. "I'm in something over my head," he said.

The confession begun that evening ended in August, 1987 when Clayton Lonetree was found guilty on all charges of espionage. Today he sits in a military prison cell, a thirty-year sentence stretching before him.

# SIX

# MEN WITHOUT CHESTS

A good many people fret themselves over the rather improbable speculation that the earth may be blown asunder by nuclear weapons. The grimmer and more immediate prospect is that men and women may be reduced to a sub-human state through limitless indulgence in their own vices—with ruinous consequences to society.

—Russell Kirk

In Clayton Lonetree's pitiful slide into treason, his commitment to the Marine creed of *semper fidelis*—always faithful—dissolved without much resistance (a fact that particularly grieves me, a former Marine). Lonetree betrayed his oath of honor not in response to torture or threats but to loneliness and boredom. Even more grievous is the fact that Lonetree's case is just one of a series of recent spy scandals in which men and women have sold their country for sex and cash.

John Walker's spy ring kept it all in the family; FBI agent Richard Miller betrayed the United States for Soviet sex and cash to pay his mortgage; CIA agent Sharon Scranage was indicted on eighteen counts of espionage after she was swept off her feet by a romantic businessman who just happened to be the cousin of Ghana's Marxist leader; and Jonathan Pollard was caught selling secrets to Israeli intelligence.

Nor are all such betrayals of trust confined to the world of espionage. In the financial world, young inside traders put their own monetary interests above their fiduciary trust; in the church, libidinous and larcenous ministers indulge their passions with abandon, and, when caught, refuse church discipline; in government, politicians cannot restrain their glandular urges long enough to run a presidential campaign, or they mortgage a nation's economic future while they play house on the Hill.

None of this is unique to our day, of course. Betrayal and corruption have existed as long as politics, religion, finance, and the military have existed. But the sheer number of recent scandals cannot help but raise strong suspicion that we are dealing with something more than just a few bad apples in the national barrel.

A *Time* cover story on ethics lamented, "What's wrong? Hypocrisy, betrayal and greed unsettle a nation's soul"; while the *Washington Post* wrote of "a society increasingly confronted by incidents in which the actions of adults or children seem bereft of morality and conscience."[1]

"Some experts say the depth of the problem has reached a point where common decency can no longer be described as common," continued the *Post.* "Somewhere, somehow, they contend, the traditional value system got disconnected for a growing number of America's next generation."[2] The *New Republic,* identifying the widespread "sense that nothing is true and everything is permitted," accuses society of a failure "to teach civilization."[3]

When the *New Republic,* the *Washington Post,* and *Time*—none of which are generally recognized as champions of conservative morality—suddenly become concerned about a decline of virtue, some line has surely been crossed. But the fact of the matter is, we shouldn't be surprised. Men and women are fallen creatures, and the decline of virtue is deeply rooted in human nature itself.

What varies from society to society, however, is the strength of internal restraints that bring this inherent depravity under control—habits informed by social stigmas and moral convictions. "Civilization is an exercise in self-restraint," said William Butler Yeats.[4] Radical individualism and its resulting relativism destroy this self-restraint.

Without reference to any standard above himself, an individual will invariably make moral choices on the basis of self-interest alone. (One is reminded of Samuel Johnson's reaction when he was informed that a certain guest believed that all morality was a sham. "Why, sir, if he really believes there is no distinction between virtue and vice," roared Johnson, "let us count our spoons before he leaves."[5]) In the absence of any commitments above self-interest, all that remains is grasping ego and the desire to maximize pleasure and minimize pain. Is it any wonder that abstractions such as duty, valor, honor, and justice cannot compete?

The treasonous embassy guard, the double-talking politician, the corrupt minister, the avaricious businessperson—all act in a logical manner, given their assumptions. Their only deterrent, after all, is the possibility of getting caught.

In a prophetic essay published in 1947, C.S. Lewis foresaw these consequences of relativism in a society. He likened the composition of the properly ordered human soul to that of the human body: the head (reason) must rule the belly (the sensual appetites) through the chest (what Plato called the "spirited element"). Since the chest is made up of "emotions organized by trained habit into stable sentiments," wrote Lewis, it is the indispensable liaison between the extremes of cerebral man, ruled only by rationality, and visceral man, ruled only by appetite.

Relativism excises this spirited element, or character, Lewis wrote, producing "men without chests." Lewis might well be describing today's inside traders, and corrupt politicians and pulpiteers. He might well be describing Clayton Lonetree: "In a sort of ghastly simplicity we remove the organ and demand the function. We make men without chests and expect of them virtue and enterprise. We laugh at honor and are shocked to find traitors in our midst. We castrate and bid the geldings be fruitful."[6]

Societies are tragically vulnerable when the men and women who compose them lack character. A nation or a culture cannot endure for long unless it is undergirded by common values such as valor, public-spiritedness, respect for others and for the law; it cannot stand unless it is populated by people who will act on motives superior to their own immediate interest. Keeping the law, respecting human life and property, loving one's family, fighting to defend national goals, helping the unfortunate, paying taxes—all these depend on the individual virtues of courage, loyalty, charity, compassion, civility, and duty.

When even one individual lacks the character and inner restraints necessary to subject his or her own passions to the common good, society as a whole is threatened. Government, laws, police, and public policies can do little to protect society against such persons. Nothing illustrates this more dramatically than the chilling tale of Gaetan Dugas.

Some studies of the AIDS crisis in the United States identify French Canadian flight steward Gaetan Dugas as Patient Zero—the initial carrier of the virus. Before his death in 1984, Dugas estimated that he had had sexual liaisons with 2,500 partners in New York and California bathhouses, rest rooms, bars, hotels, and motels. Even after doctors told Dugas he had a fatal, sexually transmitted disease, he continued to infect dozens of partners. "I've got gay cancer," he would tell them after coupling, perversely enjoying the merging of sex and death. No one knows how many victims the epidemic he unleashed will ultimately claim.

When individuals are "freed" from commitment to principle, only threat of punishment or bribery can make them subordinate their own interests for the sake of social harmony. "We can see that it is the relationship of the individual with his society that today lies at the core of our troubles," writes Henry Fairlie in *The Seven Deadly Sins Today*. "One of the corrections of Sloth is fortitudo, which is perhaps best translated as the strength of courage. Such an ideal for the citizen would have been understood in almost any other age but our own. Our societies simply do not ask this strength of courage from us, or even much force of character, and so have held out carrots, to make us do sullenly what we ought to do with devotion."[7]

But social rewards and punishments can never adequately fill the gap left by the absence of character. And in that absence, government's efforts are powerless to impose moral behavior on its citizens.

Paradoxically, however, it is to that very government that people most often turn when lack of character becomes rampant in society; it is to the state that they turn for the benefits communities no longer provide. For example, when people don't care about the homeless or the hungry, they expect government to deal with the problem. When individuals act irresponsibly or antisocially, citizens look to government to restrain them. And when democratic means fail to solve such problems or restrain such individuals—which they will, as Dugas illustrates—then the officials themselves look to any means available.

First a program is created, then a bureaucracy; in the process, the state takes on more and more power. As government swells, so does its tendency toward repression. Before long, civil rights and liberties are eliminated in an effort to control the citizenry. And thus decadent societies can pave the way for totalitarian governments; thus the relativism that seems to promise freedom can actually lead to repressive, collectivistic governmental structures.

When a culture is beset by both a loss of public values—as we saw earlier in our examination of relativism and today's intolerant tolerance—and a loss of private values—as we've seen in these examples of decadence and loss of character—the overall decline undermines society's primary institutional supports. This is a crucially important point, and one we will examine more closely.

God has ordained three institutions for the ordering of society: the family for the propagation of life, the state for the preservation of life, and the church for the proclamation of the gospel. These are not just voluntary associations that people can join or not as they see fit; they are organic sources of authority for restraining evil and humanizing society. And the family, state, and church, as well as the closely related institution of education, have all been assaulted and penetrated by the new barbarians. As we shall see in subsequent chapters, the consequences are frightening.

# SEVEN

# BARBARIANS IN THE PARLOR

The little human animal will not at first have the right responses. It must be trained to feel pleasure, liking, disgust, and hatred at those things which really are pleasant, likeable, disgusting, and hateful.

—Plato

Three-year-old Keisha was just one of the thousands of children who are victims of our society's fragmented families, but she was one of the fortunate ones. Though her young, unmarried mother lived on public assistance and her father was in prison, Keisha did have a father, of sorts. My friend Charles and his wife, who are active in pro-life and pro-family debates, had met Keisha's mother after she had sought help from a Christian counseling service, and they had become friends. Frequently Charles and his wife would bring

Keisha home with them for dinner or an occasional overnight visit. Keisha would sit on Charles's lap, happily listening to Bible stories.

"I don't have no daddy," Keisha would say to Charles.

"Oh, yes, you do," he'd respond.

"That's right," she would giggle. "You're my daddy!"

But as Keisha got a little older, she began to change. She didn't run to hug Charles when she saw him, and she wouldn't sit on his lap to do puzzles or hear stories.

"Honey, why aren't you coming to your daddy?" he asked her one day.

"You're not my daddy," she said defiantly. *I don't need no daddy.*"

In attempting to understand what lay behind this startling statement, Charles learned that Keisha's mother had attended a parental counseling session at her children's school. There a guidance counselor had applauded and affirmed the single mother's independence, autonomy, and self-sufficiency. It seemed like a good idea. But the result—"I don't *need* no daddy"—was not.

Well-meaning social workers and counselors are attempting to solve the incredible problem of family fragmentation by claiming there is no problem. After all, it's much easier to redefine the family than restore it. But when a mother is taught that she's better off without a husband, when a three-year-old is taught that she doesn't need a father, something is wrong.

With trends like this, the traditional family may soon be added to the endangered species list. Since 1970 the rate of marriages has dropped 30 percent while the number of divorces is up 50 percent. More than one million American children witness their parents' divorce each year, and ten million children now live in one-parent homes. The illegitimacy rate has doubled; over half of inner-city children are born out of wedlock.

In his excellent television documentary, "The Vanishing Family," Bill Moyers interviewed dozens of unwed mothers and teen fathers in poor urban areas. Several girls explained that they would like to work or get married, but they couldn't afford to because they would lose their welfare. A boy who had fathered six children probably spoke for many when he expressed his sense of filial responsibility with these chilling words: "Ain't no woman gonna mess up my life." Moyers despairingly concluded that the family has all but disappeared from America's inner cities.

An outbreak of crime, corruption, and chaos has resulted from this virulent breakup of the American family. Harvard professors James Q. Wilson and Richard J. Herrnstein have traced the close connection between crime and the lack of proper moral training in the home. The failure of the family to provide a model of responsible behavior has filled our city streets with young people whose only role models are pimps and pushers, and our prisons are populated by kids who follow their heroes to jail. (Or, more often, go in their place.)

The enormity of this epidemic became powerfully evident to me when I visited Rikers Island, the vast complex that houses New York City's offenders—over 20,000 prisoners. It was Easter morning, and I preached in the chapel to a few hundred inmates. Then the chaplain and I spent an hour walking the maze of concrete corridors, stopping occasionally to talk to an inmate through the small openings in the thick steel doors.

In every cell it was the same: eighteen and nineteen-year-old kids lying on their bunks staring dully at the ceiling. Few knew or cared that it was Easter. Without roots of love and security—for most were from broken families—they were connected to nothing but their needles and their gangs.

As I walked that cold cell block, I knew I was looking into the face of a new lost generation. It was a chilling scene, filled with a despair more deadly than anything ever recorded by Hemingway or Fitzgerald.

Fragmented families and rootless youth are not confined to the inner city, of course. The crisis reaches every part of our society. Who hasn't seen the packs of mall orphans cruising shopping centers to avoid returning to homes shattered by divorce, neglect, or abuse? Each year about two million young people between the ages of thirteen and nineteen attempt suicide, and between 1950 and 1977 the suicide rate among adolescents quadrupled for males and doubled for females.[1] What drives our young to such horrifying lengths? Morally impoverished, groping for love and direction, the children of Rikers Island and Main Street find evil substitutes in all the wrong places.

Who is responsible for the meltdown of America's families?

Certainly government policies must bear some of the blame. Welfare programs subsidize illegitimacy by making it more profitable for a mother to live alone than with her husband. Liberal divorce laws make changing spouses a tempting convenience when times get tough.

Society must also answer for its contribution to the problem. As our small friend Keisha could tell us if she understood it, there is considerable societal pressure for the family to be redefined. If Dad's left home and the kids feel bad, we just change the definition of what is good. Wives don't need a husband; children don't need a father. A family can be whatever the situation dictates.

This was made eminently clear several years ago when a much-heralded White House Conference on the Family was angrily protested by militant groups. The word "family" was too restrictive, they said, implying a traditional husband/wife/children/home scenario. Using the word "families" would be more inclusive, connoting any kind of cohabitational arrangement. The Carter administration renamed the meeting the White House Conference on Families.

But welfare programs, divorce laws, and societal pressure are actually the effects of much deeper causes. For the meltdown of America's families can be traced to the core of radical individualism and relativism in our society. Such self-centeredness saps the "we" from our vocabulary, says Henry Fairlie.

"It is impossible to translate 'I'm OK, you're OK' into the plural. It deliberately does not say 'We're OK,' or claim to say it, because 'we' as a unit does not command our allegiance, only separate identities in transaction with each other. In this way even the family is no longer a 'we' but an exercise in mutual therapy for the self-centered egos of its members. If any of the members, parents or child, finds that the therapy is insufficient, that it wants more massage, it is free to leave."[2]

No social contract—whether it be marriage, business, or commitment to the common good—can resist unbridled egoism. Individualists consider contracts valid only if the "commitments" are in their own best interest, says Robert Bellah. If the contract no longer meets their needs, it should be broken. Yet when the family "we" breaks down into a cacophony of competing individual voices, something vital to society is lost.

Anyone who has observed toddlers at play understands that children are not uncorrupted innocents. "We are all born charming, frank and spontaneous and must be civilized before we are fit to participate in society," declares Miss Manners, echoing Plato.[3] It is the job of the family to do this civilizing.

Ordained by God as the basic unit of human organization, the family is not only necessary for propagating the race, but is the first school of human instruction. Parents take small, self-centered monsters who spend much of their time screaming defiantly and hurling peas on the carpet and teach them to share, to wait their turn, to respect others' property. These lessons translate into respect for others, self-restraint, obedience to law—in short, into the virtues of individual character that are vital to a society's survival.

No other structure can replace the family. Without it, our children have no moral foundation. Without it, they become moral illiterates whose only law is self.

From the streets they go to the cells of Rikers Island; from the shopping malls they go to Wall Street's inside trading, committed to only one thing—looking out for number one. Loveless, lawless, lonely, these insecure and rootless youngsters go on to breed the next generation of barbarians. Thus fresh reinforcements for the invasion are born every day.

# EIGHT

# BARBARIANS IN THE CLASSROOM

The supreme end of education is expert discernment in all things—the power to tell the good
from the bad, the genuine from the counterfeit,
and to prefer the good and the genuine to the bad
and the counterfeit.

—Samuel Johnson

Standing before a huge American flag, Barbara
Walters looked sternly into the television camera. "The
alarm has sounded," she said. "The clock is ticking. But
most of us are still asleep."

Nuclear threat? Acid rain? An epidemic?

No, Walters was referring to the deterioration of
American education. Test scores are plummeting, she
said. Most high school students she surveyed thought
the Holocaust was "a Jewish holiday." Many couldn't
locate the United States on a world map. Others had

never heard of the Federalist papers.

But Walters, to her credit, probed beyond academic performance. The real crisis, she argued, is one of character. "Today's high school seniors live in a world of misplaced values," she said. They have no sense of discipline. No goals. They care only for themselves. In short, they are "becoming a generation of undisciplined cultural barbarians."[1]

We shouldn't be surprised. Modern education could not logically be expected to produce anything else.

Why? Because so-called value neutral education, which purports to teach no values, does in fact promote a value system of its own. And that system runs counter to the moral restraints essential to character.

A friend recently sent me a videotape that illustrates this clearly. Titled "Sex, Drugs, and AIDS," it was shown in her son's high school to give health information about how AIDS is transmitted and how it can be avoided. It even grudgingly mentions abstinence as a way to protect oneself.

But as the tape continues, it becomes obvious that the filmmakers had a second agenda: to teach that there's nothing wrong with homosexuality. A boy relates how he had been intolerant of gays, but after discovering his own brother had AIDS, he realized that homosexuality was just another life-style option—one that he would not judge.

Apparently the producers could not leave it at germs and antibodies. They had to get in this affirming conversion experience on the path to "enlightened" opinion. So a high school student who is taught at home that homosexual behavior is morally wrong is now taught at school that it is as viable a life-style choice as heterosexuality. This is the tolerant, value-neutral position.

Or is it?

The new barbarians who have invaded American education, as they have the news media and our legislatures, elevate tolerance as the supreme virtue. Allan Bloom calls this new tolerance "the virtue, the only virtue, which all primary education for more than fifty years has dedicated itself to inculcating."[2]

Teachers and school administrators encourage students to choose from a smorgasbord of what they term morally equivalent life-styles: homosexuality, adultery, premarital promiscuity. Gorge yourself on one or sample them all. And this smorgasbord morality, which is itself a value system, tramples on the sensibilities of any who hold to moral absolutes—particularly Christians.

"Sex, Drugs, and AIDS" is not an isolated example. A California sex education curriculum titled "Intelligent Choice of Sexual Lifestyle" advises seventh graders to set a "purely personal standard of sexual behavior" for themselves. A sex education curriculum for an *elementary* school system in the same state specifies that children will "develop an understanding of homosexuality," view films, act out homosexual roles, and take a test on what they have learned. So ten-year-olds get gold stars if they do well in homosexual role-play.[3]

Every area of education has been infected by this value-neutral philosophy. This is not only tragic but ironic, since at one time the pursuit of virtue was the specific goal of education. "If you ask what is the good of education," said Plato, "the answer is easy—that education makes good men, and that good men act nobly."[4]

Early on, our nation pursued Plato's vision. For example, a Massachusetts law passed in 1789 charged that Harvard University's professors should "exert their best endeavors to impress on the minds of children and youth committed to their care and instruction the principles of piety and justice and a sacred regard for truth, love of their country, humanity and a universal benevolence, sobriety, industry and frugality, chastity, moderation and temperance, and those other virtues which are the ornament of human society and the basis upon which a republican constitution is founded."[5]

An extraordinary list. But it is typical of higher education throughout much of American history when the goal was not to indoctrinate students in one ideology or another, but to inculcate, above all, a passion or "sacred regard" for truth.

How quaint, antiquated, and irrelevant such descriptions seem today. Voice them on almost any high school or college campus in the country and you'll be ridiculed by hooting mobs of otherwise tolerant students, egged on by professors intoxicated by the spirits of the age. Relativism and individualism have rewritten the rules of the educational game. They have "extinguished the real motive of education."[6]

This barbarian influence on education began as early as the middle of the nineteenth century with the innovative and compelling ideas of Freud, Darwin, Feuerbach, and Marx, who called into question the idea of a transcendent moral law. As a result, "During most of the twentieth century, first artists and intellectuals, then broader segments of society, challenged every convention, every prohibition, every regulation that cramped the human spirit or blocked its appetites and ambitions," says Harvard President Derek Bok.[7]

The situation has reached a point today where it is not a matter of repelling the invaders, or even holding them at bay. They have stormed and taken the citadel: "The ideologies which gained entry into the academy in the sixties claim that the fundamental intellectual principles of Western culture are illegitimate and must be overthrown. . . . The Marxists, feminists and deconstructionists have made it clear that their prime enemy is the Judaeo-Christian tradition of metaphysics. With that destroyed, terms like truth, good, evil and soul can be discarded."[8]

This atmosphere of hostile skepticism about the accessibility of truth—or even its very existence—combined with a disdain for traditional moral limits have produced a radically new educational environment. Under this new regime the university must be scrupulously agnostic about the nature of human good and must communicate this commitment to those in its care. To assert a dividing line between good and evil, or the superiority of one perspective on truth above another, would be a betrayal of the most fundamental commitment of liberal education: openness.

Allan Bloom writes: "Openness—and the relativism that makes it the only plausible stance in the face of various claims to truth and various ways of life and kinds of human beings—is the great insight of our times. The true believer is the real danger. The study of history and of culture teaches that all the world was mad in the past; men always thought they were right, and that led to wars, persecutions, slavery, xenophobia, racism and chauvinism. The point is not to correct the mistakes and really be right; rather it is not to think you are right at all."[9]

In this intellectual vacuum the content of higher education is up for grabs. "The current school system has an utter inability to distinguish between important and unimportant in any way other than by the demands of the market," says Bloom. The result, he maintains, is that "when a student arrives at a university, he finds a bewildering variety of courses. And there is no official guidance, no university-wide agreement—about what he should study."[10]

Deprived of leadership and surrounded by overwhelming skepticism, students become totally self-absorbed. "Their primary preoccupation is themselves, understood in the narrowest sense," concludes Bloom.[11] Intellectual certainty and moral growth may be unattainable, but material well-being is well within reach.

So we are left with a disturbing paradox. While higher education is better funded and more accessible than ever before, it has nothing left worth teaching. Our educational establishment seeks to instill a passion for intellectual curiosity and openness, but allows for the existence of no truth worth pursuing. In the absence of any commitment to "exert their best endeavors to impress on the minds of children and youth committed to their care and instruction the principles of piety and justice and a sacred regard for truth . . . and those other virtues which are the ornament of human society and the basis upon which a republican constitution is founded," these educators can only justify their existence in terms of career utility. As a result, our colleges and universities have become merely expensive job-training centers—steps on the ladder to material success.

Each spring these ivy halls graduate a new generation of leaders—doctors, lawyers, politicians, and MBAs— for many of whom personal advancement and "personal truth" are the only guiding principles. Shaped by the forces of individualism, these men and women without ethics go on to mold in their own image the business ethics, legal ethics, and medical ethics of our society. And some of them end up charting the course of our nation on Capitol Hill.

# NINE

# BARBARIANS IN POWER

Men no longer are bound together by ideas, but by interests; and it would seem as if human opinions were reduced to a sort of intellectual dust, scattered on every side, unable to collect, unable to cohere.

—Alexis de Tocqueville

Egypt's might is tumbled down . . .
Greece is fallen and Troy town,
Glorious Rome hath lost her crown.[1]

Ruined civilizations have always been the stuff of balladeers and bards. But the decline of a culture can never be summed up in a phrase or a stanza, and a host of causes lay buried in the rubble of the Roman world.

Near the end, Rome's agriculture and trade languished while inflation flourished. Yet the great city on the seven hills had survived such troubles in the past.

The major problem was that the empire had not been well-governed for years—not since the strong and principled leadership of Marcus Aurelius. Skill in government had long been a Roman specialty; but the cruel expedients by which later emperors tried to force revenue out of people who could not pay, while allowing those who could pay to escape, were not good government. These and other decreed devices that ran counter to Roman tradition plunged the empire into a downward spiral, until the situation alternated between anarchy and despotism.

Today we see no flames shooting out of our Capitol dome in Washington, no crashing timbers in the Oval Office. However, many observers sense in our own political processes intimations of those characteristics that surrounded Rome's decline and fall—a scent of smoke strong enough to make many uneasy.

Typical was a 1987 editorial in *The London Observer*, written back when the 1988 presidential race included thirteen candidates eagerly crisscrossing the country: "Rarely have the American people been offered so great a choice, and seldom have they had so much reason to feel depressed about it. There are probably thousands of potentially great presidents out there. But so far . . . they have all decided not to run."[2]

Most might dismiss this as simply a smug British putdown of their former colonists. But the satirical editorialist captured with uncanny accuracy a feeling many Americans share. Gone is our nation's once-unbridled confidence in the democratic experiment and our ability to meet any challenge. Instead, there is growing disillusionment with politics, reflected in steadily declining voter turnouts.

Recent political campaigns, particularly the 1988 presidential contest, have alternated between making voters angry and putting them to sleep. From scripted debates to demagogic television advertisements to glitzy photo opportunities and meatless newsbites, these campaigns inject a walloping shot of Novocain into the body politic.

What has caused this indifference, this general malaise? As with the home and the classroom, we can trace it back to the trends of relativism and individualism and the resulting erosion of individual character. Examples of this are so numerous that each day the newspapers contain fresh material. Consider just a sampling:

During the 1987 budget summit, a much-heralded effort to lasso the deficit, I asked a respected Republican senator why his colleagues weren't aggressively fighting spending increases.

"Ha," my friend replied, "remember Social Security? A few years ago we went on the line to cap Social Security increases; the Democrats beat us to death with it. This time someone else is going to have to do it. We're not going to be heroes this time."

Survival is the first law of politics, and politicians have always been adept at getting reelected. But in the continuing budget debate, to put it bluntly, it is the survival of the nation that is at stake. The stock market crash of 1987 was only a warning; continued budget and trade deficits could trigger a disastrous collapse in financial markets around the world. America's national debt has nearly tripled in the past decade, from just under one trillion dollars to nearly two and a half trillion. We are mortgaging future generations to pay for our binge.

Where are the leaders with the character to step forward and do something? Are there really no heroes?

Apparently not. Elected representatives continue to play politics as usual on Capitol Hill. In 1987 Senator Daniel Inouye responded to the fiscal crisis by tacking $250,000 onto the budget for preventing wild pigs from attacking exotic plants in Hawaii. This may or may not save any exotic plants, but it at least gives fresh meaning to pork barrel politics.[3] So does the $50,000 Representative Silvio Conte got for endive research in Massachusetts. House Speaker Jim Wright slipped $25 million into the budget for a private airport in his home district, not twenty miles away from the largest airport in America; Senator Fritz Hollings got $13 million for a privately owned dam in South Carolina; and Senator Pressler got a bundle to wash the presidents' faces on Mount Rushmore (Q-Tips are expensive these days).

Congress is notorious for this type of self-indulgence. In 1987, while decrying government spending, it allowed itself an automatic raise; a day later, when it was too late to affect the raise, the members virtuously voted against it. Thus the lawmakers got their money but could tell their constituents that they had voted against the raise. This process, or some variation of it, takes place every year. (Due to the principled resistance of a few good men and women, a similar effort to maneuver the pay raise was defeated in 1989.)

Congressman Henry Hyde's comment regarding the issue of congressional immunity from ethics is most apt: "The only thing preventing lawmakers from seeking an exemption from the law of gravity is the fact that they would have to violate the separation of church and state to pray for it."

What other than loss of character could explain the flood of insider books about the Reagan presidency? By the time the president left office, nearly a dozen of his aides had produced kiss-and-tell books about everything from Reagan's management style to his wife's astrologer to his relationships with his children. The quaint notion of honoring the trust conferred by the president of the United States is apparently no match for hefty book advances. And if money isn't motivation enough, revenge is; some, it seems, like theirs served piping hot rather than cold.

And what other than the loss of character could explain the rash of indictments of administration officials? Rather than being a place of political service, the White House seems to be a trampoline for catapulting aides into the high-rolling world of influence peddling and personal profiteering.

(I write as one intimately acquainted with Washington scandals. While Watergate's overzealous White House aides may have demonstrated that we were ready to do anything to further our party's political fortunes, the bulk of today's zealots seem to be motivated solely by the desire to further personal fortunes. The misplaced idealism of the 1970s has given way to the greed of the 1980s. The lust for power, however, remains the same.)

Lack of personal character was also responsible for scuttling the campaigns of two presidential aspirants early in the 1988 primaries. Gary Hart could not control his libido long enough to run a campaign; Joe Biden couldn't control his urge to creatively alter his resume. One long-forgotten Supreme Court nominee, Douglas Ginsburg, also bit the dust because he had, while instructing Harvard law students in upholding the law, broken the law himself by smoking pot.

Character flaws are not unforgivable, of course; we all have them. But the increasing loss of discipline and values among those who would lead us is a dangerous consequence of the rise of relativism and radical individualism in our nation. Other political consequences are more subtle, more destructive, and more ominous.

When absolutes of right and wrong are eliminated from public life, each person "does what is right in his own eyes."[4] Relativism alters the political process by transforming pluralism, one of the peculiar geniuses of the American system, into a different thing altogether.

Traditionally, pluralism meant that all conflicting values could be voiced and weighed against one another, and against a transcendent and recognized standard, in the public arena; from this healthy debate would emerge a consensus of values by which a community could be governed.

In an attempt to be inoffensively neutral, the new pluralism (born of relativism, which insists there are no objective truths), ignores all values. Consequently, nothing prevails. As Dorothy Sayers observed, "In the world it is called Tolerance, but in hell it is called Despair . . . the sin that believes in nothing, cares for nothing, seeks to know nothing, interferes with nothing, enjoys nothing, hates nothing, finds purpose in nothing, lives for nothing, and remains alive because there is nothing for which it will die."[5]

This loss of transcendent standards has also destroyed the notion of common good, so that politics has become nothing more than warfare among competing special interests. To get elected, candidates no longer appeal to the notion of any great, noble cause; instead, they woo a multitude of special interest groups, hoping to promise enough to each without offending the others.

Coalition building is politically successful, but pandering to special interests ignores any articulation or cultivation of a sense of national vision and higher purpose. In fact, it makes such vision or purpose impossible.

Once in power under this system, leaders can enact their programs only by trading between competing groups to form some sort of majority alliance. Coalition politics, as other nations have discovered, often results in paralysis. This is one reason many legislators today live in a perpetual state of frustration. Public service is no longer seen as a commission to serve the nation in the noble pursuit of the national good; instead it has become a daily balancing act between competing interest groups. As one senator described it, "Being in the Senate is like getting stuck at the airport and having all your flights cancelled."[6]

However, lest we err in blaming the problem solely on "the government," we must remember that in a democracy, people get the government they deserve. A recent poll revealed that 74 percent of the American people favor more spending on government programs; but 70 percent also oppose higher taxes. One has to conclude that the American people are either totally illogical or completely selfish: let the government do it, but don't ask me to pay for it.

If political processes seem cynical and selfish these days, it is because many citizens are cynical and selfish. If there is a loss of higher purpose among politicians, it is because there is a loss of transcendent values among the electorate. If politicians placate special interests, it is because many of their constituents see only their own special interests.

American politics simply mirrors the loss of character in the American people. If citizens are not willing to put the civic good above their own, they can't expect their leaders to do it for them. And in this way, by eroding our sense of societal responsibility, radical individualism paves the way for the death of community.

A community is a gathering of people around shared values; it is a commitment to one another and to common ideas and aspirations that cannot be created by government. As Arthur Schlesinger has observed, "We have forgotten that constitutions work only as they reflect an actual sense of community."[7]

The same individualism that has elevated the "I" above the "we" in personal relationships has elevated personal autonomy above any sense of community.

Earlier I referred to the Princeton student who demonstrated against draft registration back in 1977. His attitude proved to be a harbinger of things to come. In a recent *Rolling Stone* survey, 40 percent of the baby-boom generation said there were absolutely no circumstances under which they would be willing to fight for their country. Such selfishness from those whose fathers fought and died in World War II is not only tragic but dangerous for our country at large. "Unless people are prepared, if necessary, to die for [their nation], a society cannot long survive," says sociologist Peter Berger.[8]

Should our nation not survive, the barbarians in government and in the electorate will have done their job well, even if unwittingly. The Roman citizens who watched their empire fall probably did so with shock and sad surprise, never knowing just how it all came about or how they themselves contributed to the collapse. Future archaeologists, poking in the marble rubble of Washington, will likely say the same of us.

# BARBARIANS IN THE PEWS

Whole tracts of our religion are bare of spiritual passion, or spiritual depth. Christianity speaks the language of our humane civilization; it does not speak the language of Christ. The age, and much of the Church, believes in civilization and is interested in the Gospel, instead of believing in the Gospel and being interested in civilization.

—P.T. Forsyth

Over the past several years pollster George Gallup, Jr. has used a terse phrase to describe life in America today: "religion up, morality down." Gallup's polls indicate that 81 percent of the American people claim to be Christians. Yet, as we've seen, values devoid of Christian truth permeate American life. Would this be the case if 81 percent of our citizens were living out their professed Christian faith?

Another poll sheds light on this paradox of increased religiosity and decreased morality. According to sociologist Robert Bellah, 81 percent of the American people also say they agree that "an individual should arrive at his or her own religious belief independent of any church or synagogue."[1] Thus the key to the paradox is the fact that those who claim to be Christians are arriving at faith on their own terms—terms that make no demands on behavior. A woman named Sheila, interviewed for Bellah's *Habits of the Heart*, embodies this attitude.

"I believe in God," she said. "I can't remember the last time I went to church. But my faith has carried me a long way. It's 'Sheila-ism.' Just my own little voice."[2]

When the not-so-still small voice of the self becomes the highest authority, religious belief requires commitment to no authority beyond oneself. Then religious groups become merely communities of autonomous beings yoked together solely by self-interest or emotion.

Recently a neighbor told me how excited she was about her church. When I tried to point out diplomatically that the group was a cult, believing in neither the resurrection nor the deity of Christ, she seemed unconcerned. "Oh, but the services are so wonderful," she said. "I always feel so good after I've been there!"

Such misguided euphoria has always been rampant among those seeking spiritual strokes rather than a source of truth. But what about the church itself, that body of people "called out" to embody God's truth?

Most of the participants in Robert Bellah's study saw the church as a means to achieve personal goals. Bellah notes a similar tendency in "many evangelical circles to thin the biblical language of sin and redemption to an idea of Jesus as the friend who helps us find happiness and self-fulfillment."

These "feel gooders" of modern faith are reflecting the same radical individualism we discussed in earlier chapters. Though the need has never been greater for the church to be a repository of truth, to maintain its authority, and to hold society to moral account, it seems the church is not equal to the task. The new barbarians have invaded not only the parlor and politics but the pews of America as well.

This situation is the result of a two-fold assault: a frontal attack and subversion from within.

In recent years a flood of lawsuits has eroded religious freedoms and church authority. Suits have been filed in an attempt to inhibit everything from creches on town greens to crosses on public property to Bible studies in classrooms and private homes to prayers at high school commencements. Many have succeeded, thus steadily excising a religious presence from the public arena.

A recent case involving Washington, D.C.'s Georgetown University illustrates how this trend has affected religious liberty and the authority of church institutions. It began when a student organization, the Gay People of Georgetown University, demanded recognition and funding from the university to promote homosexual education and to sponsor gay social events. Georgetown refused, arguing diplomatically that "while it supports and cherishes the individual lives and rights of its students, it cannot subsidize this cause because it would be an inappropriate endorsement for a Catholic university."[3] The gay students sued, alleging illegal discrimination.

Under the District of Columbia's Human Rights Act, no organization can legally deny benefits to anyone based on "sexual orientation discrimination." At the initial hearing, however, the District of Columbia Superior Court sided with Georgetown, agreeing that the general constitutional guarantee of religious freedom took precedence over Washington's Human Rights Act.

The students appealed, and in November, 1987, the Court of Appeals reversed the decision, concluding that "the District of Columbia's *compelling interest* in the eradication of sexual orientation discrimination outweighs any burden imposed upon Georgetown's exercise of religion by the forced equal provision of tangible benefits" (emphasis added).[4]

Translated out of legalese, this means that the court believed guaranteeing homosexual rights was so central to government's role that it outweighed the right of religious institutions to distribute their money according to their religious beliefs. Thus a local, thirteen-member city council arbitrarily determined Washington's "compelling interest," and a local court swept aside two hundred years of constitutional protections to enforce it.

This is a frightening precedent. After all, what government bureaucracy doesn't think its own interest is "compelling"?

The Court of Appeals did affirm that Georgetown need not give formal university recognition to the homosexual group, acknowledging that the court could not determine what the university should think about homosexuality (though there was the implication they would if they could). But the judgment forced the university to further the District of Columbia's vision of equality by requiring that a Roman Catholic institution pay the bill for homosexual dance mixers. I suppose stranger things have happened; I just can't think of any.

With so much at stake, one would assume that Georgetown would appeal to the Supreme Court. It did not. The university, like a man boasting of the necktie used to hang him, proclaimed the decision a victory. Since the court did not require the university to recognize the gay group, just to fund it, Georgetown announced it had won an important point and should therefore give up the fight and set about to heal and rebuild.[5]

Georgetown contends that it stood its ground and won a partial victory. A few more victories like this, and there will be precious little religious liberty left to defend.

Whenever the state balances political interests against religious interests, the scales tip toward political interests. Apparently the courts have concluded that if religious faith motivates public action, or demands standards of behavior, or exerts any other visible influence, then it is overstepping its bounds.

The Georgetown case shows the relentless external pressures facing religious institutions and the church. It is also true, however, that the church has been crippled from within by an invasion of barbarian values and habits.

Nowhere is this more evident than in the electronic church, where lavish ministries compete for audience share and viewer dollars as surely as network programs vie for ratings and advertising dollars. There are notable exceptions, of course. Billy Graham, respected religious statesman, has used television for years to faithfully preach the gospel. But much of the electronic church has given in to the prevailing moods of the culture it purportedly exists to confront.

The very nature of television as a medium invites this. Television is immediate, visual, and dependent on its ability to entertain to perpetuate itself. Low ratings spell death for programming. Thus the need for constant emphasis on emotion, drama, and financial success—the same elements that make "Wheel of Fortune" America's most popular game show.

William Fore points out in his book *Television and Religion* that one reason the electronic church has proven so popular is that it gives religious sanction to the American tradition of self-interest. The electronic church, says Fore, corrupts "the biblical tradition so that religion itself becomes the key to maximizing self-interest, and there is no effective linkage to virtue, charity, or community."[6]

Isolated in front of their television sets, the utilitarian individualists find in much Christian programming what they seek most—the promise of material gain—now sanctified in the name of God. Meanwhile sofa-loads of expressive individualists recline in their living rooms nibbling chocolates and reveling in TV-induced tears, testimony, and titillation.

Conformity to the culture's prevailing mood is not peculiar to the electronic branch of the Christian church. In my extensive travels over the past twelve years I've met with pastors, talked with church members, and spoken in hundreds of churches. And from my observations I must conclude that the church, broadly speaking, has succumbed to many of the culture's enticements.

I don't want to generalize unjustly or be overly harsh, but it's fair to say that much of the church is caught up in the success mania of American society. Often more concerned with budgets and building programs than with the body of Christ, the church places more emphasis on growth than on repentance. Suffering, sacrifice, and service have been preempted by success and self-fulfillment.

One pastor confided to me, "I try not to talk about subjects that make people uncomfortable. My job is to make sure they come back here week after week."

Many churches are more concerned about what happens inside their doors than outside. Members will help the poor and needy as long as they don't have to dirty their own hands to do it. Admittedly, it's easier to organize fellowship suppers and church picnics than it is to reach out to the sick and suffering in the community. Caring, after all, takes time and personal involvement.

And then there is the other extreme: the churches who care more about what happens outside than inside. These trendy souls have made a head-long dash to embrace every cultural attitude and cause and drag them into the sanctuary. Consider just one example—a proposed Episcopal rite to bless homosexual marriage: "In the name of God, I, George, take you, Stan, to be my companion; and I solemnly promise here before God and these witnesses that I will stand beside you and with you always, in times of celebration and of sadness, in times of pleasure and of anger, in times of sickness and of health; I will care for you and love you so long as we both shall live."[7]

Though this proposed rite may sound "strange and shocking to many," writes the Episcopal bishop of Newark, John Shelby Spong, in his book *Living in Sin: A Bishop Rethinks Human Sexuality*, "all words that announce new life sound foreign to the ear, at least until experience illumines understanding.

"The time has surely come for the churches of America not just to tolerate, but to celebrate and welcome, the presence among us of our gay and lesbian fellow human beings," continues Bishop Spong. "One way to do that is for the church to admit publicly its own complicity in their oppression, based on its vast ignorance and prejudice . . . [by stating] its willingness and eager desire to bless and affirm the love that binds two persons of the same gender into a life-giving relationship of mutual commitment."

Bishop Spong goes on to suggest church blessings and rites for the rocky footpaths of modern romantic relationships, both hetero and homo, which affirm the "goodness of sexuality," free from the guilt the church has generated over the years. He suggests, for example, a liturgical service to mark the end of a marriage, describing one such "painful, traumatic, but intensely real" service held to "offer this all too human reality called divorce to God."

Certainly God brings healing, forgiveness, and renewal to all who confess their human failings to him with a repentant heart. But we need not offer "the reality" of broken commitments to God as if they were sacrifices of obedience.

Spong asserts: "There will always be individuals who will test the boundaries of any rule, but in our generation the rules have become so out of touch with reality that they are simply disregarded. The tide of change always begins with the trickle of a few nonconformists, and then it grows into a veritable flood as increasing numbers of people abandon the convictions of the past."

Like other tolerant intolerants of our day, the bishop loads his language, focusing on such positive notions as "celebration," "life-giving," and "commitment" in the face of the dark "prejudice" and "obsessive concern" of the church. By implication, anyone who disagrees with his ideas is "out of touch with reality."

There are, of course, thousands of churches across America that reject conformity to society and faithfully proclaim the gospel. But on balance, I fear many are unconsciously succumbing to the seductive forces of our culture and yielding the solid ground of commitment to Christ.

And into this vacuum of spiritual authority has come the New Age movement. As yuppies by the BMW-load discover that Dom Perignon, jacuzzis, and pasta machines don't produce fulfillment, they are turning to spiritual things. Not to the traditional church, however, but to the New Age movement, which is really the age-old path of Eastern mysticism, traceable to ancient Egyptian, Babylonian, and Chaldean religions. As one major book publisher put it, "Just as organized religion seemed to become more abstract and more intellectual, from left field comes this whole field of ancient practices which offer a measure of hope to the unchurched."[8]

The New Age belief system, if it can be called that in all its bizarre diversity, is not immoral but amoral. It has no absolute moral standard; instead it exalts the individual and celebrates relativism. No wonder the New Age is attracting adherents by the millions. It is the perfect religion for today's new barbarians.

Dostoyevsky wrote that anything is permissible if there is no God. How much more so if everything is God!

# ELEVEN

# THE GREAT NIGHTFALL?

But it seems that something has happened that
   has never happened before; though we know
     not just when, or why, or how, or where.
Men have left God not for other gods, they say,
   but for no gods; and this has never happened
   before
That men both deny gods and worship gods,
   professing first Reason,
And then Money, and Power, and what they call
   Life, or Race, or Dialectic.
The Church disowned, the tower overthrown, the
   bells upturned, what have we to do
But stand with empty hands and palms upturned
   in an age which advances progressively
     backwards?

                        —T.S. Eliot

We live in a new dark age. Having elevated the

individual as the measure of all things, modern men and women are guided solely by their own dark passions; they have nothing above themselves to respect or obey, no principles to live or die for. Personal advancement, personal feeling, and personal autonomy are the only shrines at which they worship.

The reigning god of relativism and the rampant egoism it fosters coarsen character, destroy any notion of community, weaken civility, promote intolerance, and threaten the disintegration of those very institutions necessary to the survival and success of ordered liberty. "We have committed what to the republican founders of our nation was the cardinal sin," says Robert Bellah. "We have put our own good, as individuals, as groups, as a nation, ahead of the common good."[1] The resulting chaos—a clamor of individual selves striving against one another—contrasts sharply with Plato's vision of the establishment of order (in the soul and in the polis) or what Russell Kirk describes as "a systematic and harmonious arrangement, whether in one's own character or in the commonwealth."[2]

T.S. Eliot said there were two ways of looking at a crumbling culture. The first says that a society ceases to be Christian when material prosperity becomes its overriding individual and corporate aim. The second viewpoint maintains that a society has not ceased to be Christian until it becomes something else. Eliot believed that the culture of his day, the 1940s, was predominantly negative yet still Christian. The choice for the future, he said, was between the formation of a new Christian culture and the acceptance of a pagan one.

I believe that the decades since Eliot wrote those words have tipped the balance. Vestiges of Christian influence still remain; but those Christian absolutes that have so profoundly shaped Western culture through the centuries are being consciously rejected by the men and women who direct the flow of information and attitudes to popular culture: communicators, educators, entertainers, and lawyers. As Eliot put it, "Paganism holds all the most valuable advertising space."[3]

This cultural crisis is all the more sinister because it is invisible to those who have already become captive to its lie. Radical individualism, which has brought us to this critical juncture, blinds most people to the fact that there is a crisis. Freed from the archaic impediments of family, church, and community, these men and women cannot see how their liberty has enslaved them to alienation, betrayal, loneliness, and inhumanity.

They've grown so accustomed to the dark, they don't even realize the lights are out.

G.K. Chesterton accurately described their plight: "There are commonwealths, plainly to be distinguished here and there in history, which pass from prosperity to squalor, or from glory to insignificance, or from freedom to slavery, not only in silence, but with serenity. The face still smiles while the limbs, literally and loathsomely, are dropping from the body. These are people that have lost the power of astonishment at their own actions."[4]

Whittaker Chambers, the skeptic turned Christian who saw our century first as a Communist spy and then as an impassioned defender of the West, died despairing: "It is idle to talk about preventing the wreck of Western civilization. It is already a wreck from within. This is why we can hope to do little more now than snatch a fingernail of a saint from the rack or a handful of ashes from the fire, and bury them secretly in a flower pot against the day, ages hence, when a few men begin again to dare to believe that there was once something else, that something else is thinkable, and need some evidence of what it was and the fortifying knowledge that there were those who, at the great nightfall, took loving thought to preserve the tokens of hope and truth."[5]

Perhaps the barbarians have already won. Perhaps the great nightfall will soon be upon us. Theologian Donald Bloesch proposes that it may be out of the utter destruction of culture that the church will emerge, phoenixlike, from the ashes.[6] We don't know.

But one thing we do know: it isn't *necessary* that such predictions come to pass. As Christians we cannot be historical determinists. There are no inexorable elements propelling history. God is sovereign over human events.

Yet it is men and women, under his jurisdiction, who write the pages of history through the sum of their choices. We never know what minor act of hopeless courage, what word spoken in defense of truth, what unintended consequence might swing the balance and change the world. "The death of a man at a critical juncture, his disgust, his retreat, his disgrace, have brought innumerable calamities on a whole nation. A common soldier, a child, a girl at the door of an inn, have changed the face of fortune, and almost of Nature," said Edmund Burke.[7]

Burke was referring to historical figures. The man who died at a critical juncture was Pericles, the Athenian general who shaped his culture; the man who retreated was Prime Minister Pitt on his retirement from public life. The child was twelve-year-old Hannibal, taking an oath to one day attack Rome; and the girl at the inn was Joan of Arc.

History pivots on the actions of individuals, both great and ordinary. In this regard one cannot help thinking of Esther, the young Israelite woman who married into royalty just when evil men were plotting the annihilation of the Jews in the fourth century B.C. Her cousin urged her to plead with her husband the king to save her people; when Queen Esther faltered, he added his famous remonstration: "Who knows but that you have come to royal position for such a time as this?"[8]

Esther prayed and found her courage renewed, despite the knowledge she might die. Advisors, friends, and officials had been executed for provoking her husband's wrath. Nevertheless she went to him leaving her cousin the message: "I will go to the king, even though it is against the law. And if I perish, I perish."[9]

Esther did not perish. Her decision to act without knowing the outcome changed the history of an entire race of people, an event still celebrated at the annual Jewish Feast of Purim.

But it is not the prospect of success nor some grand vision of changing history and saving the world that should motivate the Christian. No, it is duty alone that should compel us to act in the arena in which God has placed us.

All this being true then, the question remains: how do we respond to the invasion of the new barbarians? If the forces arrayed against us are so formidable, is there any hope?

*Part III*

# A FLAME IN THE NIGHT

# TWELVE

# GOD AND POLITICS

The church as a tool is a church of fools.
                                    —Richard J. Neuhaus

Back in 1976 many evangelicals had great hope for the reversal of America's moral decline and firm convictions about just where that hope lay. A relatively unknown candidate had emerged from Georgia to take the country by storm. His name was Jimmy Carter, and he was a Baptist who talked openly about his faith. He even taught Sunday school.

Disillusionment soon set in, however. Even a president who taught Sunday school didn't seem to make a difference. So in 1978 leaders of what is now known as the Religious Right met in Washington to set their own conservative political agenda for the 1980s. Their candidate, Ronald Reagan, would be different, they promised. His public charisma and apparent sympathy for their convictions would channel evangelical energies and change the nation.

On election night, 1980, the Washington Hilton was awash with blue balloons, white streamers, and exuberant evangelicals. Men and women more accustomed to singing "Nearer, my God, to Thee" cheered their victory lustily to "Happy Days Are Here Again." "Welcome to the Great Awakening of the 1980s," observed one commentator.

But as the sun set on the Reagan presidency eight years later, it also set on the hopes of many of these once-euphoric Christians who had overestimated their influence and underestimated the difficulty of keeping their balance on the slippery slope of politics. Despite unprecedented access to the Oval Office, they had been unable to implement their evangelical agenda. Most of the items had been either defeated or shelved.

After eight years of the most conservative presidency in recent memory, *Roe v. Wade* was still on the books. The anti-pornography campaign could claim a study commission but no legislation. Despite zealous anti-drug crusades, crack and cocaine continued to rule the streets of America; gang warfare and spiraling crime rates stalked the inner cities. And prayer-in-school advocates were left with nothing but the dubious comfort of President Reagan's assurance that "as long as there are math tests, children will pray in schools."

Even smaller local battles failed to show much effect from evangelical influence. Christian groups in Texas aggressively organized to oppose pari-mutuel racing; in Virginia they joined forces against both the lottery and pari-mutuel racing. In both Bible Belt states the referenda passed overwhelmingly.

There are several different theories about why the Religious Right failed. Some say evangelicals simply aren't monolithic as a voting bloc, as Pat Robertson discovered in his sputtering campaign for president. Others believe that earnest religious people were simply betrayed by double-talking politicians. And still others question whether there ever was a mandate for social change. Perhaps the great moral revolution of 1980 was wishful thinking; advocates fell into the trap of believing their own propaganda.

But I think the true explanation lies in our disregard for these two key truths: first, the solutions to all human ills do not lie in political structures; and second, it is impossible to effect genuine political reform solely by legislation.

Many Christians, like much of the populace, believe the political illusion; that is, that political structures can cure all our ills. The fact is, however, that government, by its very nature, is limited in what it can accomplish. What it does best is perpetuate its own power and bolster its own bureaucracies. Government programs to help the needy, for example, easily get hung up in their own red tape—tangled in forms and memos and committees and meetings and budget analyses.

As historian Paul Johnson observed in *Modern Times*, the twentieth century is the pathetic story of the effort to live by the bread of political power alone. In not-so-modern times, Samuel Johnson saw the same truth: "How small of all that human hearts endure / That part which kings or laws can cause or cure."

Christians cannot afford to continue to confuse access to the Oval Office with political influence; nor can we put all of our hopes and energies in the political basket. Invitations to White House dinners don't assure political pull; nor can politics promise the penetrating societal change we seek.

In their high expectations of politics, many Christians also misjudge the source of true societal reform. In reality, it is impossible to effect genuine political reform without reforming individual and, eventually, national character.

While it has a moral responsibility to restrain evil, government can never change the hearts and minds of its citizens. Attitudes are forged by spiritual forces, not by legislation. "All history, once you strip the rind off the kernel, is really spiritual," said historian Arnold Toynbee. Values change when spiritual movements stir the hearts of people and when fresh winds of reason stir their minds.

As we've seen in earlier chapters, such standards as keeping the law, respecting human life and dignity, loving one's family, defending one's nation, helping the needy, and sacrificing for the common good depend directly on individual virtues such as courage, loyalty, charity, compassion, and duty. The success of government itself depends on these characteristics; yet government is powerless to create them in its citizens. Real social changes cannot take place unless a nation's character demands them.

"Politics is the art of the merely possible," argues Russell Kirk. "The long-run decisions of the electorate are formed not by party platforms and campaign speeches, but by visions—by prejudices, if you will. Only the changing of such visions can produce large enduring political alterations, for better or worse."[1]

Not that I advocate withdrawal from politics. I believe every aspect of life is subject to Christ's lordship and that Christians are called to bring biblical influence to every part of society, including political structures. That's my objective when I speak before state legislatures and other political groups, urging reforms in our criminal justice system. We are to work within and without politics for justice and righteousness.

And we cannot abandon the political arena because progress there is elusive, excruciatingly slow, or even nonexistent. We must dig in for the long haul. It took decades to bring about the abolition of slavery, to end industrial abuses, and to establish civil rights. Those who led the battles for these reforms were sometimes dismayed, but not deterred. We should take courage from them; but we must do so without illusions.

British Prime Minister Margaret Thatcher is an unusual politician in that she understands—and is willing to state publicly—the limits of politics.

Addressing the General Assembly of the Church of

Scotland, Mrs. Thatcher said, "The truths of the Judaic-Christian tradition are infinitely precious, not only, as I believe, because they are true, but also because they provide the moral impulse which alone can lead to that peace...for which we all long....There is little hope for democracy if the hearts of men and women in democratic societies cannot be touched by a call to something greater than themselves. Political structures, state institutions, collective ideals are not enough. We parliamentarians can legislate for the rule of law. You the church can teach the life of faith."

Our ultimate hope, even for politics, does not lie within the political realm. It lies in the reassertion of what Margaret Thatcher calls the *moral impulse.*

"When all is said and done, a politician's role is a humble one. I always think that the whole debate about the church and the state has never yielded anything comparable in insight to that beautiful hymn 'I vow to thee my country.' It begins with a triumphant assertion of what might be described as secular patriotism, a noble thing indeed in a country like ours: 'I vow to thee my country all earthly things above; entire, whole and perfect the service of my love.' It goes on to speak of 'another country I heard of long ago' whose King cannot be seen and whose armies cannot be counted, but 'soul by soul and silently her shining bounds increase.'

"Not group by group or party by party or even church by church—but soul by soul. And each one counts."[2]

There are no quick fixes. Politics alone cannot hope to cure our ills. Only what Russell Kirk calls "the changing of vision," what Margaret Thatcher calls "the moral impulse," can change the character of an increasingly secularized nation.

# THIRTEEN

# MORAL EDUCATION

All sober inquirers after truth, ancient and modern, pagan and Christian, have declared that the happiness of man, as well as his dignity, consists in virtue.

—John Adams

The moral impulse. I can't think of a better definition for those internal restraints that are the very substance of character. Margaret Thatcher expressed it beautifully and concisely with that phrase, followed by her admonition that the task of the church is to "teach the life of faith." We are to restore the moral impulse to a nation whose selfish impulses have led it down a road of corruption and decline; we are to reawaken those internal restraints on passion and self-interest. In short, the task of the church—our task—is *moral education.*

Moral education is not a matter of tacking the Ten

Commandments on schoolroom walls or making college freshmen take Introduction to Character 101. You cannot drill character the way you drill multiplication tables.

Moral sensibilities are based on a complex range of beliefs and experiences that stretch back into earliest childhood; these roots of the moral ordering of the soul are nourished by relationships with parents and friends, by community traditions, by role models, by the emulation of heroes in literature or history, by a whole series of early choices that create moral habits. Human nature, formed by a million factors and experiences, is not easily shaped by some moral instructor. We are more complex than we imagine.

> Below the surface-stream, shallow and light
> Of what we *say* we feel—below the stream
> As light of what we *think* we feel—there flows
> With noiseless current strong, obscure and deep
> The central stream of what we are indeed.[1]

Aristotle made an important distinction relevant to this point. There are, he argued, two kinds of virtue. The first is intellectual virtue, which is the cerebral process of discovering truths through instruction and study and the application of reason in philosophy, literature, and history. The second is moral virtue, which is more fundamental and is the product of habits learned early in life from family, class, and community. Moral virtue teaches the values of courage, justice, self-restraint, seriousness, and compassion. "A man's habits become his virtue," said Edmund Burke.[2]

Moral virtue without intellectual virtue may be inarticulate, unable to produce a systematic justification for its convictions. But moral virtue remains the prop that holds up the social order by controlling passions that would otherwise require a repressive apparatus of law enforcement.

Intellectual virtue without moral virtue, however, is an exercise in hypocrisy. Robespierre, the austere lawyer who led the Jacobins of the French Revolution, was selfless in his dedication to the revolution, uncompromising in his principles. His admirers called him "the voice of virtue." Such purely intellectual virtue, cut off from the habits of the heart, became the cold, hard virtue of the guillotine, exacting and merciless with an insatiable taste for blood.

Moral virtue is the most essential element of a just society. But once squandered, can it be restored? Who or what is equipped to regenerate a moral impulse in the long-atrophied conscience of a corrupt culture?

Perhaps it's easier to answer such questions by starting with the negatives, which sum up the points we have discussed thus far.

First, we cannot expect moral virtue to spring from academe. No social institution is more captive to culture's relativism than today's value neutral education. Even in a best-case scenario—even in the context of a belief in absolutes—education is no provider of moral virtue. It can inculcate a passion for truth, informed by history and tradition. It can communicate a faith that the universe is so constituted that it yields truth to those who seek it with tenacity. But colleges and universities, as Russell Kirk has noted, "cannot make vicious students virtuous or stupid students wise, but they can endeavor to prove to their students that intellectual power is not hostile to moral worth, and they can aspire to chasten intellectual presumption with humility."[3]

Second, while government has a worthy task to perform and depends for its success on citizens of character, it can do little to create them. By upholding a standard of justice and enforcing the rule of law, the state does provide a limited form of moral education. By punishing some acts and rewarding others, it reinforces certain basic moral habits that are necessary to the peace and order of society. But humanity's deepest motivations, its strongest virtues and blackest vices, escape the control of government. Any government.

Neither Stalin nor Calvin could dictate character. To believe government can do so is to perpetuate an illusion and to invite tyranny. As writer Orestes Brownson replied to Karl Marx in 1848: "In most cases the sufferings of people spring from moral causes beyond the reach of government, and they rarely are the best patriots who paint themselves in the most vivid colors, and rouse up popular indignation against civil authorities. Much more effectual service could be rendered in a more quiet and peaceful way, by each one seeking, in his own immediate sphere, to remove the moral causes of the evils endured."[4]

And finally, we cannot look to the media as a disseminator of moral virtue, no matter how many Christians get jobs at CBS. Television, the most popular medium of our day, is so limited in its ability to present any coherent vision, any message other than fleeting emotion, that it is a handicapped resource even at its best.

We cannot pin our hopes for the future of moral education on the classroom, on legislation, or on the airwaves. No, I believe there are only two institutions that can cultivate moral virtue: the family and the church, those "communities of memory" to which Robert Bellah refers, where traditions, history, and discipline provide a context for understanding the world. The enduring strength of our society lies in strengthening these two communities.

The family is the primary and most important source of moral instruction. Russell Kirk does not exaggerate when he argues that "Our very nature is acquired within families: we are not self-reared after the fashion of Tarzan. The human family lacking, there would cease to be a human nature. Doubtlessly some race resembling in outward aspect the extinct *homo sapiens* would survive for a time. But you and I would feel little kinship with these . . . degenerate caricatures of human beings among whom families had ceased to exist."[5]

We've seen all too clearly in the West that when

radical individualism fragments the family, it fragments the transmission of manners and morals from one generation to the next, breaking the fragile chain of instruction that upholds society by instilling moral virtue. No matter how we try to compensate, it is nearly impossible for those left drifting at this stage to catch up later. (There is no makeup exam in moral instruction.) Unable to hand down our moral heritage, we raise generation after generation of increasingly rude, lawless, and culturally retarded children.

How can the family be strengthened? Certainly there are some practical steps: Welfare reforms must be extended and augmented by volunteerism and help from the private sector. Divorce laws should be tightened. Laws requiring fathers to support their children should be enforced; and increased tax deductions for children would ease financial pressures on families.

But ultimately the recovery of the family will depend upon something much more fundamental than tax policies and welfare reform. The problem will only be adequately addressed when we deal with the individualism and relativism that are destroying the notions of duty and commitment central to the marital and familial bond. And in this regard, the most crucial thing we can do is also the quietest—and the most difficult.

We must strengthen our commitment to model strong families ourselves, to live by godly priorities in a culture where self so often supersedes commitment to others. And as we not only model but assertively reach out to help others, we must realize that even huge societal problems are solved one person at a time.

Real help for troubled urban families, for example, will come only through individuals who care. That may mean volunteering to tutor inner-city kids, to teach young mothers about nutrition, or to help young fathers develop a sense of responsibility.

One example of this type of volunteerism is Prison Fellowship's Project Angel Tree, one of our programs that excites me most. Since 1982, Angel Trees have provided Christmas gifts for hundreds of thousands of inmates' children as well as needy families in urban areas. Christian volunteers follow up with these families, getting them involved in local churches, assisting them with material needs, and providing friendship and models of Christian love. Such individual caring has helped to reconcile shattered families and to gently bring restoration to some of the most broken and seemingly hopeless situations.

The second important instructor of moral education is the church. At its best, the church is a community where virtue is taught and celebrated, where character is instilled through instruction and discipline. It can inculcate values that adhere to a transcendent standard of right and wrong, equipping Christians to live out the truth in love in the midst of a relativistic and lonely culture.

For hope and victory in the battle against the barbarians, Christians need not look to new organizations, newsletters, charters, or conferences and speakers. Such efforts are worthy, but limited in what they can accomplish. This new dark age will be best illumined, I believe, by character and hope transmitted through those structures God ordained long ago: the family, the first school of human instruction and the best building block of society; and the church, the community called by God to love him and to express that love in service to others.

If we are faithful, these will light the way back to eternal things.

# FOURTEEN

# PARADOX

Civil society was renovated in every part by the teachings of Christianity. In the strength of that renewal, the human race was lifted up to better things. Nay, it was brought back from death to life.

—Pope Leo XIII

Before Rome's fall, its citizens had lost the characteristics that had made them distinctly Roman: discipline, respect, and obedience. Incest and adultery had invaded many families, breaking the natural bonds of love and commitment and setting yokes of bitterness, disdain, and hatred in their place. Moral education had been supplanted by indolence, corruption, and decadence.

Thus damaged from within, Rome was unable to resist direct barbarian assaults from without. The once-great empire fell in the fifth century, and Rome was sacked by the Visigoths, a Germanic tribe whose cavalry proved superior to the foot soldiers who had sustained and advanced the Roman Empire for centuries. During the next few centuries, chaos ruled Europe. Warring bands of illiterate Germanic tribes opposed and deposed one another. Cities and cultural centers disappeared as inhabitants were scattered across the land in crude huts and rough towns. Literacy, law, and order—the pillars of civilization—crumbled, and the aristocratic culture of the ancient Western world nearly disappeared. Early medieval Europe seemed destined for complete barbarism.

One force prevented this. The church.

Instead of conforming to the barbarian culture of the Dark Ages, the medieval church modeled a counter-culture to a world engulfed by destruction and confusion. Thousands of monastic orders spread across Europe, characterized by discipline, creativity, and a coherence and moral order lacking in the world around them. Monks preserved not only the Scriptures but classical literature as well; they were busy not only at their prayers but in clearing land, building towns, and harvesting crops. When little else shone forth, these religious provided attractive models of communities of caring and character; and in the process they preserved both faith and civilization itself.

During the seventh century while corruption flourished in France under the Merovingian kings, the clergy were "the ablest, best educated, and least immoral element in Gaul," states Will Durant. The

French monks ran schools and labored to transmit both literacy and moral teaching to the masses. The bishops sheltered orphans, widows, paupers, and slaves. They opened hospitals, constructed aqueducts, banned witchcraft, and were respected by a population staggering under the greed and dishonesty of their political leaders.

In Ireland, the great saints Columba and Columbanus organized monasteries throughout the land. Their novices illuminated manuscripts and converted pagans "with the Bible in one hand and classic manuscripts in the other," notes Paul Johnson. They cleared forests, plowed fields, fasted, prayed, and lived lives of vigorous discipline. Columbanus, who had read Virgil, Pliny, Horace, Ovid, and Juvenal, preserved arts and scholarship along with the Scriptures.

In England the religious orders fought illiteracy, violence, lechery, and greed. They drained swamps, bridged creeks, cut roads; they copied manuscripts, organized industrial centers and schools. By holding on to such vestiges of civilization—faith, learning, and civility—these monks and nuns held back the night, and eventually the West emerged from the Dark Ages into a renewed period of cultural creativity, education, and art. The barbarians could not withstand this stubborn preservation of civilization.

It is important to note that the church challenged not only the values of the barbarians but those of the Roman Empire as well. Living by a value system dictated by the kingdom of God, they rejected both

Roman and barbarian lapses of character, uprooting such attitudes as the aversion to physical labor predominant among the Roman masses and the barbarian love of violence. As points of light in a dark age, they called attention to the values of an endless age. And in so doing, they saved their civilization.

Though the world now appears far more sophisticated than when the Visigoths overran Rome, it's only because today's barbarians wear pinstripes instead of animal skins and wield briefcases rather than spears. Like the monastic communities of the Middle Ages, the church today can serve as outposts of truth, decency, and civilization in the darkening culture around us. For even though the church itself is shot through with an individualism that cripples its witness, even though the church today—like the medieval monastic communities—is made up of sinners like you and me, it is the one institution in society that still has the capability to challenge culture by bearing witness to God's transcendent standards of absolute justice and righteousness.

Why? Because the church has an independent locus of authority beyond itself, beyond the state, beyond the tides of passing fashion. The true church cleaves to the absolute standards of Scripture and is infused with the work of the Holy Spirit to guide it.

I refer, of course, not to any particular denominational body, but to the church as the body of Christ: what the apostle Peter called "the holy nation"; what the Apostles' Creed calls "the holy catholic church." It is that community of God's people of every race spread around the globe which makes visible the kingdom of God in the midst of the kingdoms of this world.

Historically, as Roman Catholic historian Christopher Dawson has pointed out, the church has been the soul of Western civilization. And that is the church's role today: to take its stand as the main line of resistance against the new barbarians and to provide culture with a new sense of moral vision.

But it is crucial that we pause here to emphasize and understand a great paradox: if the church is to fulfill its role, if the church is to do anything at all useful for culture, if the church is to resist and conquer the barbarian invaders, the church must first disregard all these objectives and concentrate on being faithful to its identity in Jesus Christ. *The church must be the church.* That is its first duty.

If we set out to recapture culture, seeing the church as God's instrument to save the world, we will fail, just as the conservative Christian political movement has failed; just as liberal Christian social movements have failed. The church is not a tool to rebuild society.

Our goal is to be faithful to the holy God who calls us to be the church, whether we actually make a difference in our world or whether it falls to pieces around us and dissolves into a stew of secularism. We seek to be the church for no other reason than that it is our calling from God. We defend the independence and faith of the church because it is the body of Christ, the locus of spiritual authority, the bride preparing for the coming of the Groom.

In anticipation of our Master's return, Christians are to be committed to biblical obedience, which means working for justice and righteousness, serving as advocates for the needy and powerless who cannot speak for themselves. When we are faithful to the challenges of Matthew 25 or the prophetic exhortations of Amos, we cannot help but make a positive impact on society.

But, again, this is not *why* we are faithful. We are motivated not by a desire to make an impact on society but by obedience to God's Word and a desire to please him. When our goal becomes success rather than faithfulness, to invert Mother Teresa's maxim, we lose the single-minded focus of obedience and any real power to actually succeed.

For years the slogan of the National Council of Churches was "the world sets the agenda for the church." This sounds socially relevant; but in fact it displaces God, who long ago set his own agenda for his church: obedience.

Only when the church abandons its worldly pretensions does it gain its greatest influence, says Richard John Neuhaus. "The church best serves the world when it is most distinctively and most unapologetically the church ... when the church dares to be different, it models for the world what God calls the world to become. The church models what it means to be a community of caring and a community of character."[1]

This is not to suggest for a moment that the church should turn its back on the world or retreat to monastic outposts. I would be the first to argue that we have a duty to proclaim the truth, to act as salt and light, to hold the world to moral account. It's all a matter of motivation. When we act out of social or political motives, we can easily become frustrated. But when we act out of pure obedience, then God may well use the church to profoundly influence social and political structures.

Christopher Dawson has traced the impact the faithful church can have, arguing that historically the church has provided the principal dynamic of social change in the West only when it has been most distinctly and unapologetically the church. He notes that the monastic communities served as a pattern that has been repeated in the history of the West. From that pattern it is clear that positive cultural change, such as the end of the Dark Ages, comes not from a synthesis of Christianity and culture but from a tension between the two. Without this stimulation from a transcendent perspective, no court of appeal stands above the existing order, providing a reason and dynamic for change.

Implicit in Dawson's viewpoint is the assumption that culture and society are less than ultimate, less than autonomous. Cultural progress is a process of continual conflict, a series of battles that must be fought.

When the church transcends culture, it can transform culture. In the Dark Ages, reform did not arise from the state but from communities of those who remained uncompromising in a compromising age. As Dawson notes, "It is only in Western Europe that the whole pattern of culture is to be found in a continuous succession and alteration of free spiritual movements; so that every century of western history shows a change in the balance of cultural elements, and the appearance of some new spiritual force which creates ideas and institutions."[2]

The lesson across the centuries is clear. The survival of Western culture is inextricably linked with the dynamic of reform arising from the independent and pure exercise of religion—from the moral impulse. But this lesson also raises sobering questions.

Is the church ready to take on this mantle? Are we really able to be a church that transcends culture? What will it take to set us apart?

# FIFTEEN

# METANOIA

A world of nice people, content in their own niceness, looking no further, turned away from God, would be just as desperately in need of salvation as a miserable world—and might even be more difficult to save.

—C.S. Lewis

The monastic orders of the Dark Ages could not have modeled communities of character if they had looked like the troubled world about them. Today, in a new age darkened by the collapse of character and the dissolution of faith, the church cannot model the kingdom of God if it is conformed to the kingdoms of man.

Too often in recent years the church has suffered from the same collapse of character that is so widespread in our culture. Too often the church has been apathetic, marked by individualism, and constrained by the love of self rather than the love of Christ.

If the church today is to be the church, it must diligently protect its spiritual integrity. This begins with what the Greeks called *metanoia*, which means a "change of mind" and is translated in the New Testament as "repentance."

Repentance is commonly thought of as simply an acknowledgment and confession of sin. Surely we as individuals need to repent of our disunity, our moral laxity, our hard hearts—indeed, we need to repent of the sins of the society of which we are a part. But the repentance God desires of us is not just contrition over particular sins; it is also a daily attitude, a perspective.

Repentance is the process by which we see ourselves, day by day, as we really are: sinful, needy, dependent people. It is the process by which we see God as he is: awesome, majestic, and holy. It is the essential manifestation of regeneration that sets us straight in our relationship to God and so radically alters our perspective that we begin to see the world through God's eyes, not our own. Repentance is the ultimate surrender of self.

It was not by accident, I suspect, that the first of the Ninety-five Theses Martin Luther nailed to the Wittenberg church door read, "When our Lord and Master Jesus Christ said 'repent,' He willed that the entire life of believers be one of repentance."

The call to repentance is one of the most consistent themes of the Old and the New Testaments. The Old

Testament recounts kings falling before God, pleading for mercy, as we see most eloquently in David's prayer of contrition in Psalm 51; and repentance was the central message of God's prophets.

Repentance is, as J. Edwin Orr has put it, "the first word of the Gospel." It is the centerpiece of John the Baptist's message. "Repent and believe" were Jesus' first words in the account of Mark, and his last words to the disciples commanded them to preach repentance and forgiveness of sins.

"The Christian needs the church to be a repenting community," proclaims Richard Neuhaus. "The Christian needs the church to be a zone of truth in a world of mendacity, to be a community in which our sin need not be disguised, but can be honestly faced and plainly confessed because we know that the worst word about us as sinners is not the last word. The last word is about us as sinners forgiven."[1]

Christians are to repent of sin, both individually and as a body. One of my favorite examples of the church becoming this type of repentant community comes from the Philippines and a man who has become a dear friend.

Over the years, Jaime Cardinal Sin, Archbishop of Manila, watched with growing dismay the swelling corruption of Ferdinand Marcos's dictatorial regime. He prayed long over this suppression of human liberty and the plight of his nation.

After the assassination of Benigno Aquino, the archbishop knew he had to act. But what should he do?

As he studied his Bible, he saw in the Old Testament accounts of Israel's corrupt leaders a pattern he felt applied to his own nation. *When God wants to punish a people,* he reasoned, *he gives them unjust rulers.* What the people of the Philippines needed was not a call to revolt against their unjust ruler but a call to repent of their own unjust hearts.

Archbishop Sin spent months crisscrossing his homeland, preaching repentance, conversion, and obedience. He called the Filipinos to prayer and fasting; the people responded by organizing Bible studies and prayer groups. A wave of revival—of holiness and renewal—swept through the Philippines. According to some reports, hundreds of thousands began to meet in small groups to fast and pray for their nation. These Christian citizens became the foot soldiers for a non-violent revolution, and the eventual result was the peaceful ousting of Marcos and the restoration of a democratic government.

I'm not suggesting that God blessed the Philippines because the people repented; it would be presumptuous to assume we could so neatly understand the mysteries of God's dealings with modern nations. Rather, my point is simply that Jaime Cardinal Sin understood that the church's fundamental responsibility is to renew its own integrity and to be a repentant community. *The church must be the church.*

No less mysterious than God's dealings with nations is the inexorable operation of his Holy Spirit in the lives of individuals. When a person repents—changes his or her mind—God takes control of even the most indomitable spirit. No one exhibits this more clearly and dramatically than G. Gordon Liddy, as colorful a character as any Hollywood director could order up from Central Casting.

This former White House aide has probably sparked more controversy and inspired more fascination than any of his Watergate cohorts. Even as a youth, Liddy was unconventional, to say the least.

A sickly child, he was easily frightened, he resolved to conquer his fears by facing them down. Because he feared heights and electricity, for example, Gordon would climb to the top of electrical towers. Because he feared rodents, he roasted and ate part of a rat. He exercised his will to the point where it was stronger than anything he confronted.

Liddy went on to become a pilot, an FBI agent, an attorney, a White House aide—in just a few short years. A student of Nietzsche, the German philosopher who venerated the will to power as the highest of human goals, Liddy saw the world as a challenge to be conquered. Even as the Nixon White House tumbled around him, Liddy would not be broken.

Eventually Gordon was sentenced to twenty-one years in prison for his role in Watergate. And when I visited him there, he was as tough and unrepentant as ever. As he tells it in his autobiography, titled, of course, *Will*: "Chuck asked me if I had 'seen the light.' 'No,' I replied. 'I'm not even looking for the switch.'"

Liddy served four years and was released. Greeted

by the ubiquitous press, he gave an extensive statement—in German. The befuddled journalists scratched their heads. It turned out Liddy was quoting Nietzsche.

Gordon returned to his family and started several successful businesses. He became a popular lecturer, a folk hero of sorts. He even took his act on screen, playing a part on the ultimate macho show, "Miami Vice."

One evening Liddy was a guest on the David Letterman show. "What happens after we die?" Letterman asked.

"We are food for the worms," responded Liddy.

"That's all?" asked Letterman.

"That's all," said Liddy.

Gordon Liddy had conquered every challenge set before him and moved on. But his off-the-cuff remark about death stayed with him. It made him uneasy, and he didn't know why.

Then Liddy and his wife moved to a different state, and in the process renewed a friendship with former FBI colleagues he had known for thirty years. Liddy had always been drawn to these people; they were intelligent, compassionate, well-read. So when they asked him to study the Bible with them, he agreed— but only after spelling out his terms. "I'm an agnostic," he said. "I'm here because I'm interested in the Bible. Period. Please do not try to convert me. I don't want to be bothered."

Liddy, you see, felt no compelling need for God in his

life. His interest in the Bible was purely historical. But then he thought about his friends and their thirty-year example of Christian love and excellence. "If they are persuaded of the correctness of this," thought Liddy, "then maybe I should take another look."

He started by thinking about God. "By definition, God is infinite, and by definition we are finite," he reasoned. "It is contrary to the rules of logic for a finite being to be able to apprehend the infinite. So ... there has to be some communication. That infinite being is going to have to tell me. I am never going to be able to apprehend that myself."

The next step in Liddy's reasoning was to wonder if there was any communication. Then, he says, "a light went on in my head. *That's* what this Bible is all about!" Not merely a historical record, but God's means of communicating with finite man.

But, he thought, it would be impossible for a finite being to be worthy of the infinite. So there must be not only communication but something more. So, says Liddy, "you have God sending down his Son to do two things: to win for you all of that which we cannot win for ourselves; and to continue the communication."

Many people, says Liddy, experience a "rush of emotion" in conversion. Yet for him there came a "rush of reason." He realized Christ was who he claimed to be, and Gordon Liddy became a Christian.

Since then, the man who wrote *Will* has said, "Now the hardest thing I have to do every single day is try to decide what is God's will, rather than what is my will.

What does Jesus want, not what does Gordon want. And so the prayer that I say most frequently is, 'God, first of all, please tell me what you want—continue the communication. And second, give me the strength to do what I know you want, what your will is, rather than my own.' I have an almost 57-year history of doing what I want, what my will wants, and I have to break out of that habit into trying to do the will of God."[2]

Thick theological treatises may explain doctrine, but none capture the essence of *metanoia* better than Gordon Liddy's simple words: to subordinate one's will to the will of God. And this from a man who spent his entire life affirming the indomitability of his own will.

Gordon Liddy's faith in Christ and his return to the Roman Catholic church have been as colorful and, at times, as controversial as the rest of his life. Yet I now pray for Gordon as a brother in Christ—and pray that the fruits of repentance will spill out of his life, as the grace of God has already changed his heart and will.

Without this kind of radical change of mind, there can be no conversion. There may be spiritual stirrings, inklings of interest, but unless there is metanoia, God has not been allowed to take control. An unrepentant Christian is a contradiction in terms.

Repentance is a rare message in today's church because it requires confrontation with an uncomfortable subject—sin. And sin does not sell well in our feel-good culture. When sin gets personal, people get skittish. Only the conviction of personal sin, however, brings us to Christ.

G.K. Chesterton observed that the doctrine of original sin is the one philosophy empirically validated by 3,500 years of human history. Certainly the Middle East, South Africa, Central America, Northern Ireland, and the streets of America testify to that fact. Yet we are not sinners because we sin; we sin because we are sinners. Unless the church recognizes this and preaches it, there is no way it can be a strong model of an alternative community of character to a culture corroded by sin.

# SIXTEEN

# THE WILD TRUTH

There are an infinity of angles at which one falls,
only one at which one stands.

—G.K. Chesterton

A group of scholars met a few years ago to discuss
and determine the authenticity of Christ's statements
in the Gospels. One by one Jesus' words were considered; each debate concluded with the scholars
solemnly raising slips of colored paper they had been
given. A red slip meant the statement under consideration was "authentic"; pink meant "probably
authentic"; black meant "not authentic."

The Beatitudes and the Sermon on the Mount took a
beating in the balloting. "Blessed are the peacemakers"
was swiftly voted down. "Blessed are the meek" got
only six timid red and pink votes out of the thirty cast.
In all, only three out of twelve assorted blessings and
woes from Matthew were deemed authentic.

We might dismiss this exercise as merely a party game of liberal scholars with not enough to do, except for the fact that these folks were serious. What they did must not be taken lightly, for it represents an attitude that has subtly invaded the personal lives of many in the evangelical sector of the church today. Though often ingeniously camouflaged, it is the tendency to put Scripture on our terms rather than God's, applying the parts we like and ignoring those we find too hard to handle.

If we are to be Christians whose hearts beat and break with the rhythm of the heart of God, we must take on his whole Word wholeheartedly. That means reading the Bible, studying it, committing it to memory, allowing his words to dwell richly in our minds. It means understanding Scripture in its historic, classical context. It means accepting Christ as Savior and allowing his rule to permeate our thoughts, decisions, and actions.

If the church is to be the church in a darkening age, it must take its stand on the solid ground of biblical revelation and the historic confession of Christian truth. Another word for this is orthodoxy or dogma. While it seems the dry and dusty stuff of theologians, dogma is actually the only bulwark that allows the church to both judge itself and stand fast against the currents of cultural trends. Secularism advances, theologian Donald Bloesch argues, only as orthodoxy retreats. As surely as we yield the ground staked out for the church, the barbarians will advance to claim the terrain.

In some segments of the church the battle for orthodoxy seems already lost. Politically progressive Roman Catholics appear more concerned with voicing their less-than-expert opinions on trendy issues like economic and defense policy than on defending church doctrines. Many Protestant evangelicals are becoming similarly politicized, along with some liberation theologists who have never seen a revolution they didn't want to join. Still others wrap pop psychology in Christian jargon, creating misty-eyed disciples of positive thinking.

I'm reminded of E.B. White's comment: "People have recut their clothes to follow the fashion. . . . People [have] remodeled their ideas too—taken in their convictions a little at the waist, shortened the sleeves of their resolve, and fitted themselves out in a new intellectual ensemble copied from a smart design out of the very latest page of history."[1] When slavery to fashion invades the church, our latest ideas are yesterday's fads. We adopt the world's agenda—just a few years too late. Many churchmen sport theological bell-bottoms.

Respect for dogma is not likely to endear us to the relativistic culture we seem so intent upon pleasing, however. Orthodoxy often requires us to be hard precisely where the world is soft, and soft where the world is hard. It means condemning the homosexual life-style and being labeled bigots. It means caring for AIDS patients though many think us fools. It means respecting the rule of law though our culture is increasingly lawless. It means visiting the prisoners who offend that law though our culture would prefer to forget them. In every way that matters, Christianity is an affront to the world; it is countercultural.

Defense of orthodoxy begins with a respect for the authority and inerrancy of Scripture. God's definitive revelation in Jesus Christ is given authoritative witness in the Bible, which is, for the Christian, the source of orientation and guidance. Martin Luther referred to the Word of God as "greater than Heaven and earth, yea, greater than death and Hell, for it forms part of the Power of God and endures everlastingly."[2] John Calvin argued that "We owe to Scripture the same reverence which we owe to God."[3] Pope Leo XIII insisted that "Divine inspiration not only is essentially incompatible with error but excludes and rejects it absolutely and necessarily."[4]

Earlier in this century biblical criticism and theological speculation seemed to have turned against orthodoxy. Respected critics dated New Testament documents hundreds of years after the events they recount. Most of the Old Testament was seen as ancient fables, and some scholars denied that Jesus lived at all.

Today the situation is quite different. British historian Paul Johnson began a recent lecture by saying, "Christianity, like the Judaism from which it sprang, is a historical religion, or it is nothing. It does not deal in myths and metaphors and symbols, or in states of being and cycles. It deals in facts."[5] He then outlined expert archaeological evidence supporting the historical claims of the Old Testament, followed by the over-whelming textual support for the early dating and reliability of New Testament documents.

A papyrus fragment of John's Gospel can be dated no later than the early second century, and eighty papyrus fragments exist from the second to fourth centuries. By comparison, the earliest dated manuscripts of Aristotle's *Poetics* are from the eleventh century, 1,400 years after his death. (Isn't it strange that the authenticity of Jesus' words are constantly challenged, while no one questions Aristotle?) Such findings cannot prove Christianity deductively, of course. But, as Johnson affirms, "It is not now the man of faith, it is the skeptic, who has reason to fear the course of discovery."[6]

Orthodoxy begins with the Bible, but it does not end there. It is possible for a person to believe in an inerrant or infallible Scripture and still espouse odd heresies. Ask a Jehovah's Witness or a Christian Scientist—or an Arian or a Pelagian.

Christian orthodoxy is properly defined in the context of a tradition determined by the continuity of essential doctrine, traced through a long line of theologians and saints, guaranteed by the work of the Holy Spirit. We cannot approach the Scriptures as though the Council of Nicea never met, as though Augustine and Aquinas never wrote, as though Luther never preached. While Scripture is our authoritative source, tradition acts as an authoritative guide to biblical interpretation.

Nor is orthodoxy uniquely Protestant or Catholic—or Orthodox. It is, instead, what C.S. Lewis called "mere Christianity": that which we have received from our fathers; that which was outlined in the earliest creeds and rules of faith; and that which is preserved—if not observed—in every major tradition of the church.

This is not to say that denominational differences are not important. I, for one, would not want an ecumenism that achieved its goals by watering down traditional doctrinal distinctions. Convictions concerning eschatology, ecclesiology, and the sacraments are worth our passionate commitment.

Though we must not abandon our distinctives, we can celebrate our common faith contained in the Scriptures, defined and transmitted in separate but ultimately related traditions of orthodox confession. We can confidently, vigorously, and boldly defend Christian dogma in an exercise that can draw us together in unity even as we acknowledge our differences.

The defense of orthodoxy is not tedious. It is exhilarating to live our faith unflinchingly and defend the truth fearlessly, avoiding the traps of passing fads. Chesterton likened the equilibrium necessary to do so to one who gracefully and accurately drives a team of madly rushing horses: it is "one whirling adventure; and in my vision the heavenly chariot flies thundering through the ages, the dull heresies sprawling and prostrate, the wild truth reeling but erect."[7]

# SEVENTEEN

# COMMUNITIES OF LIGHT

If my account of our moral condition is correct, we ought to conclude that for some time now we too have reached the turning point. What matters at this stage is the construction of local forms of community within which civility and the intellectual and moral life can be sustained through the new dark ages which are already upon us. And if the tradition of the virtues was able to survive the horrors of the last dark ages, we are not entirely without grounds for hope.... We are waiting not for a Godot, but for another—doubtless very different, St. Benedict.

—Alasdair MacIntyre

To model the kingdom of God in the world, the church must not only be a repentant community, committed to truth, but also a holy community.

The Judeo-Christian heritage is distinguished from all other religions by its covenant with a personal God who chose to dwell in the midst of his people. "I will dwell among the Israelites and be their God," said the Lord.[1] In Hebrew the word *dwell* meant "to pitch a tent"; God said he would pitch his holy tabernacle in the midst of the tents of the Israelites. In the New Testament we read "the Word became flesh and dwelt among us." Here also the word *dwelt* in the Greek is translated "to pitch a tent." The covenant, both old and new, is that the God of Abraham, Isaac, and Jacob, the God who later became flesh in Christ, actually dwells in the presence of his people. And thus it is that the central requirement of our faith is that we be holy, for a holy God lives in our midst.

The apostle Peter echoed this theme when he said: "You are a chosen people, a royal priesthood, a holy nation, a people belonging to God."[2]

The church is to be a community reflecting God's passion for righteousness, justice, and mercy. When we are that holy community, we make an impact on an unholy world, no matter how desperate the circumstances.

Thousands of such communities of light exist around the world in accountable fellowships where the gospel is faithfully proclaimed and where members reach out in an effort to bring God's mercy and justice to those around them. But my most vivid impressions of the church shining forth have come from some of the darkest places on earth—from prisons around the world. In some ways these fellowships bear real similarity to the monastic outposts—believers faithfully preserving the gospel as those around them sink into depravity.

One such community of light is in Zambia. There in an old colonial-era stockade emaciated inmates, wearing only loincloths, are crowded into primitive, filthy cells where they have to take turns sleeping, since there is not room for them all to lie on the floor at the same time. At night the prisoners are given a bucket of water; after they drink the water, the same bucket is used to carry off their waste in the morning.

When I visited this prison, I was with Rajan, a Christian brother and former inmate at that prison, now chairman of Prison Fellowship Zambia. He led me to a maximum-security compound within the main block. "Listen," he whispered as we got closer. "They're singing."

Guards unlocked a pair of heavy gates, and we stepped into a dusty courtyard ringed by tiny cells. There to welcome us were sixty or seventy radiantly smiling inmates; they stood at the end of the yard before a whitewashed wall, singing praises to God in beautiful harmony. Behind them on the wall was a huge charcoal drawing of Christ on the cross: Jesus the prisoner who shared their suffering and gave them hope and joy in this awful place, where they had come to Christ.

I've seen this same holy, joyous community in Latin America. There, in the midst of great political upheaval,

God is building his church in the most unlikely place—
the prisons.

Several years ago I visited Peru's Lurigancho, the
largest prison in the world, arriving just a few days after
a riot in which several nuns had been taken hostage by
the prisoners; one had been killed. The prison had since
been closed to visitors, its outer perimeter sealed by
government troops. After some lively negotiations, we
were given permission to go inside, although the
guards refused to accompany us.

The first block was six stories high, with open sewers
in the concrete floor. Angry stares followed us as we
walked from cell to cell. Then, on the second tier, a man
jumped up, grinning broadly, and pulled me into his
cell. It was clean and neatly swept, a vivid contrast to
the mess in the cellblock. He pointed proudly to a
certificate on the wall, then to his own chest, shouting,
"Me, me!" It was a graduation certificate from a Prison
Fellowship seminar. I spoke no Spanish and he no
English, but it didn't matter. We grabbed one another
in a fierce hug of Christian fellowship.

Prison Fellowship had conducted a seminar just a
few weeks earlier. Then when our volunteers were
temporarily shut out of the prison during and after the
riot, the inmates had continued the Bible study themselves. As I toured the block I came to other cells of light
in that dark place, where the smiles of Christian
inmates told the story of their utter transformation. The
dramatic contrast of this community of gentle Christians, loving and encouraging one another in this hole

of violence and hatred, was unforgettable. It was light shining in the darkness.

That light shines in U.S. prisons as well. During a riot at Washington, D.C.'s Lorton prison complex, inmates torched several buildings; armed, menacing gangs roamed the grounds. But in the main prison yard a group of Christian inmates stood in a huge circle, arms linked, singing hymns. Their circle surrounded a group of guards and prisoners who had sought protection from the rioting inmates. These Christians were a community of light, and lives were saved.

In prison, the contrast is sharp between dark and light. Choices for Christian inmates are usually clear-cut. Yet most of us in the mainstream of Western culture live in shades of gray. It's comfortable to adopt the surrounding cultural values. Yet stand apart we must.

For as the church maintains its independence from culture, it is best able to affect culture. When the church serves as the church, in firm allegiance to the unseen kingdom of God, God uses it in this world: first, as a model of the values of his kingdom, and second, as his missionary to culture.

The monks and nuns of the Dark Ages acted out of obedience to God, and God used their faithfulness—without their knowing it—to preserve culture and ultimately to restore Western civilization. As Christopher Dawson has said: "The culture-forming energies of Christianity depended upon the Church's ability to resist the temptation to become completely identified with, or absorbed into, the culture."[3] Only as the church maintains its distinctiveness from the culture is it able to affect culture.

Another example that clearly illustrates this comes from the Cuban Isla de Pinos, from a prison so dark and remote that most of the world never even knew it existed. The huge circular cellblocks were built during the 1930s under Batista's regime. When someone asked the dictator why he had built it so big, he replied, "Ah, don't worry. Somebody will come along who will manage to fill it up." That somebody was Fidel Castro.

One of the prisoners there was a young anti-Communist named Armando Valladares. Early in his confinement, he often heard prisoners—fellow Christians—taken to the firing squad. Such executions always took place at night, and the dark silence would be broken by triumphant shouts: *"Viva Cristo Rey! Long live Christ the King!"* Then the explosion of gunfire—and silence again. Soon all prisoners were gagged before their executions. The killers could not stand their victorious defiance.

According to Valladares, the most faithful member of that tiny Christian community, made up mostly of Catholics, was a Protestant prisoner known simply as the Brother of the Faith. He constantly sang hymns to God and shouted encouragement to his brothers to have faith, to follow Christ to the end.

Then one night several prisoners were forced from their cells, and guards began to beat them with sticks, truncheons, bayonets, and chains. "Suddenly," writes

Valladares, "as though to protect them, there appeared a skeletal figure with white hair and flaming, bizarre eyes, who opened his arms into a cross, raised his head to the invisible sky, and said, 'Forgive them, Lord, for they know not what they do.' The Brother of the Faith hardly had time to finish his sentence, because as soon as he appeared [the lieutenant] ordered the guards to step back ... he fired his AK submachine gun. The burst of fire climbed the Brother of the Faith's chest, up to his neck. His head was almost severed, as though from the blow of an ax. He died instantly."[4]

Fortified by the faithfulness of this one man, as well as by his own faith, in a way he could not forget, Armando Valladares survived gross inhumanity, psychological abuse, and torture for twenty-two years. In 1983 he was released and made his way to the West and freedom. His memoirs of those dark years, *Against All Hope*, have exposed to the world the hidden horrors of Castro's prisons.

And therein lies the irony: Though Castro controls the Cuban press, suppresses the visible church, conquers academia, and rules a ruthless government, he cannot rule the spirits of those he has enslaved. He cannot extinguish the light of the soul set free by God. And out of a flicker of light in one dark prison came the indictment of his regime that shocked the world.

Is this not the way our Lord works? Out of brokenness and foolishness come wholeness and might. Out of prison comes power—real power—that defies even the most brutal repression. Out of tiny monastic outposts come education, moral endurance, and artistic excellence that can save a civilization. And out of holy obedience today, in communities of light, will come what he wills, as we are faithful.

# EIGHTEEN

# THE CHRISTIAN MIND

When principles that run against your **deepest** convictions begin to win the day, then **battle is** your calling, and peace has become sin; you must, at the price of dearest peace, lay your convictions bare before friend and enemy, with all the fire of your faith.

—Abraham Kuyper

It's all well and good to sound the call for the long-term restoration of virtue: the instilling of character, the creation of moral vision, the modeling of communities of light in the dark. A few generations, or a few hundred years, and maybe our new dark age will dawn into a new morning.

But, you ask, what about today? Even as I write, unjust laws are being written, new medical technologies threaten human life, and political cowardice mortgages our future. We cannot ignore immediate concerns like these. We must bring what Harry Blamires calls "the Christian mind" to today's political and social issues. Even as we live in the perspective of eternity, warfare in the trenches is part of our duty as citizens and believers. For if Christianity is true, then it has application for all of life, and we must seek to examine all things temporal in light of the eternal. If we concern ourselves solely with "matters of faith," we talk only to ourselves.

A few years ago the editor of a major U.S. newspaper told me he had added several religion writers to his staff. "Look at the religion page," he said enthusiastically. "We're doubling the coverage!" He apparently assumed that in doing this he was doubling his witness for Christ.

But just writing or thinking about religion isn't the same as making a Christian impact on our culture. Pollsters tell us that fifty million Americans say they are born again. No doubt about it, religion is up. But so are practices unremittingly opposed to the truth of Christianity: one out of every two marriages is shattered by divorce; one out of three pregnancies ends in abortion. Homosexuality is no longer considered deviant or depraved behavior; it is an alternative life-style. Crime continues to soar: in "Christian" America there are one hundred times more burglaries than in "pagan" Japan.

Sin abounds in the midst of unprecedented religiosity.

Why?

If there are so many Christians in the U.S., why aren't we affecting our world?

I believe it's because many Christians fall into the same trap my editor friend did. We treat our faith like a section of the newspaper or an item on our "Things to Do Today" list. We file religion in our schedules between relatives and running. It's just one of the many concerns competing for our attention.

Not that we aren't serious about it. We go to church and attend Bible studies. But we're just as serious about our jobs and physical fitness.

The typical believer, says Harry Blamires, prays sincerely about his work but never talks candidly with his non-Christian colleagues about his faith. He is only comfortable evaluating his spiritual life in a "spiritual" context. This results in a spiritual schizophrenia as the Christian bounces back and forth between the stock market and sanctification.

Such categorizing would be plausible if Christianity were nothing more than a moral code, an AA pledge, or a self-help course. But Christianity claims to be the central fact of human history: the God who created man invaded the world in the person of Jesus Christ, died, was resurrected, ascended, and lives today, sovereign over all.

If this claim is valid—if Christianity is true—then it cannot be simply a file drawer in our crowded lives. It must be the central truth from which all our behavior, relationships, and philosophy flow.

Blamires describes our dilemma well: "As a thinking

being, the modern Christian has succumbed to secularization. He accepts religion—its morality, its worship, its spiritual culture; but he rejects the religious view of life, the view which sets all earthly issues within the context of the eternal."[1]

As a result of our failure to apply Christian truth to all of life, the secular mind-set monopolizes public debate.

One revealing example of this occurred several years ago when the respected *Journal of the American Medical Association* published "On the Physical Death of Jesus Christ," an article describing the medical causes of Christ's death. Within days the magazine had received an avalanche of angry letters attacking it for publishing such slanted drivel. One writer accused the journal of "disguising theological, we dare say, fundamentalist biases."

This seems a rather hysterical response to what few, Christian or pagan, would discount as historical fact. Whether he was the Son of God or not—the article did not assert that Christ was resurrected—there was a historical figure named Jesus who was crucified. But the extreme reaction shows how aggressively the secularists will defend their monopoly.

The problem is that Christians often allow this reaction to intimidate them. We withdraw from the battle, spending most of our time safely talking with each other, venturing out of our burrows only to conduct evangelistic outreach. And thus we fail to bring the Christian mind or perspective as a counterpoint to the prevailing secular assumptions. We allow them to define modern values unchallenged.

As Charles Malik, Christian scholar and former president of the United Nations, has said, "The problem is not only to win souls, but to save minds."

Christians must contend for truth; not simply by quoting Scripture, which our secular neighbors don't believe anyway, but by presenting persuasive arguments. I've been fortunate to have opportunities to do this in the criminal justice arena.

Since crime rates are soaring, prisons overcrowded, and new prison construction tremendously expensive, a number of state legislatures have invited me to speak in recent years. One invitation came from Texas, which has some of the worst prison crises in the nation.

When I arrived to speak, the chamber of the House of Representatives was in a state of near-anarchy. Some legislator was speaking, but no one was listening. His colleagues were milling about in noisy clusters or talking on the telephones installed at each desk. The only people paying attention were the school civic classes packing the galleries to watch democracy at work. (If you have ever seen a legislature in session, you know it is one of the minor miracles of democracy that it has survived nonetheless.)

The Speaker of the House welcomed me, but warned, "Mr. Colson, I hope you can get their attention. George Bush was here three weeks ago and the whole time they just kept doing what they're doing."

Thus encouraged, I took the podium and began to speak—rather loudly. The roar continued for a few minutes. Then several groups started filing to their seats. Then a few more. Finally the whole place was listening attentively. (Politicians, I have discovered, have a growing interest in prisons—sometimes a very personal interest!)

I told them why restitution rather than prison is the best response for nonviolent offenders, mentioning that it can cost $80,000 to build a cell and $16,000 a year to keep a person locked up—about the same as sending them to Harvard. Under restitution programs, nonviolent offenders pay back their victims, at minimal cost to taxpayers, and are less likely to repeat their crimes.

Afterward I was escorted to a small anteroom where fifteen or twenty representatives came to talk with me. Several commented, "What you say makes sense. Where did you get that idea?" To which I couldn't help but reply, to their considerable surprise, "Have you got a Bible? Open it to Exodus 22."

I don't suggest that we can simplistically apply Old Testament civil law to modern circumstances; that is the error of the theonomist. Rather, informed by a biblical perspective along with history, right reason, and tradition, we can bring the Christian mind—and the badly needed alternatives it provides—to today's issues.

"There is no [longer a] Christian mind," asserts Harry Blamires. Nothing could more profoundly alter the character of our culture than for the millions who claim to be Christians to demonstrate the contrary.

# NINETEEN

# THE MORAL IMAGINATION

All great systems, ethical or political, attain their ascendancy over the minds of men by virtue of their appeal to the imagination; and when they cease to touch the chords of wonder and mystery and hope, their power is lost, and men look elsewhere for some set of principles by which they may be guided.

—Russell Kirk

Pomp and splendor marked the rule of Napoleon Bonaparte. Hundreds of thousands of troops did his bidding. His name was on the lips of the French people. Military strength and political power were the fruits of his victories.

But Napoleon, probably the greatest military genius of his time, knew that the world was not ultimately moved by power. "Imagination rules the world," he declared.

Societies are not held together by rules and laws; order cannot be enforced by swords or guns alone. People must find their motivation and meaning in powerful ideas—beliefs that justify their institutions and ideals.

To put it another way, societies are legitimized by "myth," using the word not to connote fictions peopled by unconventional characters, but in the sense of grand images, ideas, and words with the emotion and power that "inspire[s] people to acts of commitment and sacrifice—in the extreme case, even the sacrifice of life itself."[1]

Such myths take many forms. They can be as practical as proverbs and folk wisdom or as complex as systems of thought rooted in philosophy, science, or religion.

Confucianism, with its emphasis on just rule, piety, family, and hard work, has provided just such an appeal to the imagination and has sustained China and other Eastern cultures for thousands of years. The potent myth of communism has led millions of its followers to die in jungles, rice paddies, and rain forests with its promise of equality and brotherhood. The Western myth of liberty under law grips imaginations in cultures as diverse as the Philippines, Poland, and South Korea.

Men and women will live and die for ideas, images, and visions like this. "The real conflict in our age is between opposing types of imagination—or, to speak more accurately, among a variety of types of imagination...," says Russell Kirk. "We may perceive there, competing, the moral illusions of the fanatic ideologue, the bleary-eyed voluptuary, and the militant atheist. So the great contest in these declining years of the twentieth century is not for human economic interests, or for human political preferences, or even for human minds—not at bottom. The true battle is being fought in the Debatable Land of the human imagination. Imagination does rule the world."[2]

If imagination really does rule the world, then how can the world be changed?

I wrote earlier of the enormous complexity of the moral impulse. The same can be said of the process of accepting a worldview. People don't pick a vision or myth about the world piecemeal, as they might pick a bouquet of flowers in a garden. They come to such convictions within the framework of a broader set of historical assumptions and ideals—more like accepting a story, with all of its internal rules and consistencies.

And just as beliefs are not selected one at a time (what might be called the salad-bar theory of decision-making), longheld beliefs do not fall one at a time. In the absence of a deeper conversion of perspective—an appeal to the imagination—minds are rarely changed on single policy matters, no matter how persuasive our arguments.

For a person to switch positions on abortion, for example, he or she must make mental readjustments that go far beyond consideration of the fetus. A complex personal history and a whole structure of belief about the nature of freedom, the value of human life, the scope of individual autonomy, and the role of law must be transformed.

Plato argued that this deeper conversion of perspective was almost like an awakening—like remembering something you forgot a long time ago. It is the realization: "That fits. That is the way things should be." It is a sense of recognition. Something responds not only in your head but in the deeper layers of your being. The process is rational, but it is also aesthetic and emotional.

Which brings me to the heart of the challenge we face. For even if we confront the new barbarians, even if we seek to model communities of light, even if we think and act as Christians in a hostile culture—even all of this may not reverse the deeply ingrained cultural presuppositions of our day.

Changing the habits of a darkening age may require something far grander than our individual efforts, something beyond the reach of most of us. It may require the subtle yet rich transmission of ideas and perspectives—artistic, emotional, rational—that have provided the strong fiber for Western societies of the past. Taken together, these form a new vision to which people respond. History has seen it work in earlier times.

The closest I've come to finding a label for this process is to term it "the moral imagination," an Edmund Burke phrase filtered to me through Russell Kirk: "It is a man's power to perceive ethical truth, abiding law. . . . Without the moral imagination, man would live merely from day to day, or rather moment to moment, as dogs do. It is the strange facility . . . of discerning greatness, justice, and order, beyond the bars of appetite and self-interest. . . . It is the combined product of intuition, instinct, imagination and long and intricate experience."[3]

In contrast to the irrational imagination of Rousseau, the moral imagination values reason and recognizes truth. It asserts that the world can be both understood and transformed through the carefully constructed restraints of civilized behavior and institutions. In contrast to the utilitarian imagination of Mill, the moral imagination respects a moral law authored by God, enshrined in nature, which calls people to duties beyond themselves. In contrast to the historical forget-fulness of modernity, the moral imagination cherishes the past. It assumes that to approach the world without the companionship of the ideas of earlier times is an act of hubris—in essence, claiming the ability to create the world anew, dependent on nothing but our own pitiful intelligence.

But the moral imagination is more than rational. It is poetic, stirring long-atrophied faculties for nobility, compassion, and virtue. Imagination is expressed through symbols, allegories, fables, and literary illus-trations. Art in the service of the moral imagination can ennoble.

This is not an ideology. An ideology begins with discontent and sets out to force the universe into some speculative, rational plan. It aims at utopia by tinkering with social conditions. Marx espoused an ideology.

In contrast, the moral imagination begins with awe, reverence, and appreciation for order within creation. It sees the value of tradition, revelation, family, and community and responds with duty, commitment, and obligation. It humbly claims but limited insights into the rich and diverse perspective of orthodoxy and attempts to communicate that vision in the language and symbols of our time.

Here and there in the history of the West there have been people or communities that appealed to revealed truth, struck the chord of the moral imagination, and thereby transformed not only policies and practices but a whole manner of thought. Obvious examples are Augustine, Aquinas, and Calvin. In more recent times one could point to such writers as C.S. Lewis, J.R.R. Tolkien, and Charles Williams, who were equally fluent in debate and allegory. Or the Oxford Movement in England, which challenged the tired skepticism of the times with a rebirth of articulate conviction. Or G.K. Chesterton, who as poet, journalist, novelist, and debater championed a vigorous and joyful orthodoxy. Or T.S. Eliot, who, as the most prominent poet of his age, shocked the world by his conversion and vocal defense of Christian culture. Or Dorothy Sayers, whose wit and writing articulated the intellectual fruit of a lively commitment to Christ. Or Aleksandr Solzhenitsyn, who writes of spiritual freedom with the passion born of suffering.

Such men and women did not merely engage in controversy, though they seldom turned down a good argument. Instead, they presented a new perspective; they told a new story. They provided an alternative to the rotting myths of modernity; they presented a compelling vision of the good.

Furnishing the wardrobe of the moral imagination is not limited to people of letters, of course. This preserve belongs to all men and women of self-denial and sacrifice who both articulate and model a radically different set of personal and cultural priorities. One could point to John Wesley, who coupled a concern for holiness with a vision for social justice. Or General Booth, who reached out with martial zeal to those drowning in poverty and spiritual blindness. Or Mother Teresa, who ministers to the outcast and the dying in the gutters of Calcutta.

Pope John Paul II embodies this capacity in his courage, his deep personal holiness, and his extraordinary gift for communication. Using vivid symbols to convey an orthodox vision, he is a model of moral imagination. When he visited the prison cell of the man who had tried to kill him, publicly forgiving and embracing the guilty one, the pope displayed the radical power of Christian forgiveness before a watching world. When he pulled his hand away from the Sandinista official Father Miguel D'Escoto as the rogue priest attempted to kiss his ring, the pope embodied the church's refusal to compromise with tyranny. When he visited and preached in a Lutheran church on the five hundredth anniversary of Martin Luther's birth, Pope John Paul II evoked the unity to be found in Christ.

The moral imagination can even be found in politics. In the 1930s, England was permeated with a debilitating defeatism and pacifism. Millions of soldiers had been lost to the gas warfare and trenches of World War I. In reaction, both left and right vigorously supported appeasement and concession to Hitler. The Oxford Union debating society overwhelmingly approved a resolution that it would "in no circumstances fight for King and Country." A pledge, known as the Oxford Oath, was taken by students and teachers across the country using the same language. The Cambridge Union voted 213 to 138 for "uncompromising" pacifism. The nation was dispirited and, with the steady advance of Nazi tyranny, isolated.

Even as Hitler's limitless ambition became undeniable, some spoke of further concession. Then came whispers of surrender. "An embodiment of fading Victorian standards was wanted: a tribune for honor, loyalty, duty, and the supreme virtue of action; one who would never compromise with iniquity, who could create a sublime mood and thus give men heroic vision of what they were and what they might become," says William Manchester.[4]

The man equal to that task was Winston Churchill. On June 18, 1940, as France fell and Britain stood alone, the Prime Minister spoke to the nation: "Upon this battle depends the survival of Christian civilization.

Upon it depends our own British life, and the long continuity of our institutions and our Empire. . . . Hitler knows that he will have to break us on this island or lose the war. If we stand up to him all Europe may be free and the life of the world may move forward into broad, sunlit uplands. But if we fail, then the whole world . . . will sink into the abyss of a new Dark Age made more sinister, and perhaps more protracted, by the lights of perverted science. Let us therefore brace ourselves for our duties, and so bear ourselves that if the British Empire and its Commonwealth last for a thousand years, men will still say: 'This was their finest hour.' "[5]

Churchill imposed his "imagination and his will upon his countrymen," idealizing them "with such intensity that in the end they approached his ideal and began to see themselves as he saw them." In doing so, "he transformed cowards into brave men, and so fulfilled the purpose of shining armour."[6] Through the power of words and images, Churchill led a nation to fight for king and country—a nation that had pledged never again to fight and die on foreign fields of war.

By appealing to the moral imagination, men and women like this have been able to truly affect societal attitudes and alter the course of human events. And it is on this level that the battle for Western culture's survival will be ultimately won or lost.

That being said, I cannot in a few brief paragraphs launch a single-handed recovery of the moral imagination. But I will venture to suggest a few things that might form the parameters of a new vision.

*First, we must reassert a sense of shared destiny as an antidote to radical individualism.*

Individuals are not merely autonomous pleasure-maximizers. We are born, live, and die in the context of communities, and it is only in these communities of worship, self-government, and shared values that we discover appropriate human ends.

"Perhaps life is not a race whose only goal is being foremost," comments Robert Bellah. "Perhaps enduring commitment to those we love and civic friendship toward our fellow citizens are preferable to restless competition and anxious self-defense. Perhaps common worship, in which we express our gratitude and wonder in the face of the mystery of being itself, is the most important thing of all. If so, we will have to change our lives and begin to remember what we have been happier to forget."[7]

*Second, we must adopt a strong, balanced view of the inherent dignity of human life.*

Aversion to or disregard for the elderly, the handicapped, and the unborn is one of the surest signs of cultural degradation. And by this standard our culture has already surpassed the grim excesses of Rome and the cruelties of the barbarians who invaded it. All the traditional restraints on inhumanity seem to be crumbling at once—in our courts, in our laboratories, in our operating rooms, in our legislatures. The very idea of an essential dignity of human life seems a quaint anachronism.

As Christians, we must be unequivocally and un-apologetically pro-life. We cannot concede any ground here. We may be called to implement this in different ways, but we are all called to defend the cause of the weak, the helpless, the defenseless.[8]

*Third, we must recover respect for tradition and history.*

We must reject the arrogance of intellectual fad and fashions—the rootless reasonings of the moment. "We often read nowadays of the valor or audacity with which some rebel attacks a hoary tyranny or anti-quated superstition," said Chesterton. "There is not really any courage at all in attacking hoary or anti-quated things, any more than in offering to fight one's grandmother. The really courageous man is he who defies tyrannies young as the morning and super-stitions fresh as the first flowers."[9]

Cultivating the moral imagination in the frozen ground of twentieth-century skepticism is not easy, but we must keep trying. Our future depends on it.

As Russell Kirk has written, "There must appear among us men and women endowed with the sort of imaginative power that transforms the spirit of the age. . . . Adversity may strengthen character, and grim circumstances may quicken wits. Providence operates ordinarily through human agents, whose thoughts and actions may reverse the whole drift of their times.

"One thing we can do is this: to refrain from choking up the springs of the moral imagination. If we stifle the sense of wonder, no wonders will occur amongst us."[10]

May God grant us the grace, even in a darkening age, to see the wonders.

# TWENTY

# AGAINST THE NIGHT

I said to the man who stood at the gate of the Year, "Give me a light that I may tread safely into the unknown." And he replied, "Go out into the darkness and put your hand into the hand of God. That shall be to you better than light and safer than a known way."

—Minnie Louise Haskins
quoted by King George VI
Christmas broadcast, 1939

Speaking Christian truth, serving as the faithful church in a new dark age, sparking the moral impulse and stimulating the moral imagination—all these sometimes seem to be losing battles, doomed efforts. It is difficult to think of fresh beginnings in times that seem so much like the end.

We may indeed be approaching midnight. But if

there is any hope, it is to be found in a renewed and repentant people possessed of a moral vision informed by Scripture, respecting of tradition, and committed to the recovery of character. We must be a people of conviction, prepared to offer the world a story filled with courage, duty, commitment, and heroic effort— that will inflame the moral imagination of the West.

Will we succeed?

Perhaps.

Does it matter? In one sense, yes, of course. In another sense, not really. For our duty is clear no matter what the outcome.

G.K. Chesterton once wrote a long ballad about King Alfred of England. Defeated in a series of battles against barbarian invaders, Alfred was left entirely alone—his army lost, his strength broken. His situation seemed hopeless, defeat certain.

Then Alfred is visited by a vision that exhorts him to the Christian view of victory, defeat, and hope, in contrast to the determinism and despair of the "wise men" of his day, the men of the East.

The men of the East may spell the stars,
And times and triumphs mark,
But the men signed of the cross of Christ
Go gaily in the dark.

The men of the East may search the scrolls
For sure fates and fame,
But the men that drink the blood of God
Go singing to their shame.

The wise men know what wicked things
Are written on the sky,
They trim sad lamps, they touch sad strings,
Hearing the heavy purple wings,
Where the forgotten seraph kings
Still plot how God shall die.

But you and all the kind of Christ
Are ignorant and brave,
And you have wars you hardly win
And souls you hardly save.

I tell you naught for your comfort,
Yea naught for your desire,
Save that the sky grows darker yet
And the sea rises higher.

Night shall thrice night over you,
And heaven an iron cope.
Do you have joy without a cause,
Yea, faith without a hope?[1]


Can the new barbarians be resisted? I hope and believe so. It has happened before.

But even if they are not, we must go forward in obedience, in hope, even in joy. For those who are "signed of the cross of Christ go gaily in the dark."

This is the challenge—and the promise—before us.

# SELECT BIBLIOGRAPHY

I CLAIM NO GREAT ORIGINALITY for the thoughts contained in this book. They are rooted in the unflinching insights of a number of exceptional thinkers—authors, poets, and academics who have chosen to face a stern reality rather than remain in a pleasing but deceptive dream.

It is to their works that I would direct anyone who wants to look further into the issues raised by *Against the Night*. Though this list is far from exhaustive, it includes the key works that have contributed to the central themes of this book.

For a general overview, Russell Kirk's *The Wise Men Know What Wicked Things Are Written on the Sky* (Washington, D.C.: Regnery Gateway, Inc. 1987) offers a brilliant cultural critique that includes just the right balance of realism and hope. Malcolm Muggeridge's *The End of Christendom* is another good starting point—a book that effectively skewers the vanity and pretensions of the "Christian" West with characteristically caustic wit. Carl F.H. Henry's *Twilight of a Great Civilization* (Westchester, Ill.: Crossway Books, 1988) provides an insightful indictment of American neopaganism and a call for responsible Christian cultural activism. And Aleksandr Solzhenitsyn's *A World Split Apart* (New York: Harper and Row, 1978)—the commencement address he delivered at Harvard University—is a stinging, prophetic denunciation of the material obsession and spiritual poverty of the West.

Aside from these more general works of cultural criticism, a number of important books deal specifically with the social effects of relativism and individualism. Robert Bellah's *Habits of the Heart* (Berkeley: University of California Press, 1985) is must reading for anyone concerned about the consequences of rampant individualism on social institutions like the church and family. Paul Johnson's *Modern Times* is an ambitious analysis of how relativism has worked itself out in twentieth-century history. C.S. Lewis' *Abolition of Man* (New York: The Macmillan Company, 1947) is undoubtedly the best introduction to relativism's disastrous consequences on both education and morality. Allan Bloom's *The Closing of the American Mind* (New York: Simon and Schuster, 1987) covers some of the same ground from a different perspective with particular focus on higher education. And for those of a more philosophic bent, Alasdair MacIntyre's *After Virtue* (Notre Dame: University of Notre Dame Press, 1981) traces in detail the disturbing moral and political consequences of what he calls emotivism—the inability to decide any moral question except through private emotion and public power.

# AFTERWORD

WHEN CHUCK COLSON WRITES about Christians joined together in communities of light in the midst of darkness, when he speaks about the church *being* the church in a skeptical society, the ministry of Prison Fellowship is never far from his mind. While Christians are called to demonstrate the values of the kingdom of God in a variety of roles, prison ministry has been the particular arena to which God has called Chuck. And in it he has seen the victory and vitality of the church in direct confrontation with darkness.

God planted the seed of prison ministry in Chuck Colson's heart during his imprisonment for a Watergate-related offense. During his seven months behind bars, Chuck realized that the prisoners he met there, and hundreds of thousands like them, needed to know about the transforming power of Jesus Christ. They needed to hear the Truth; then they needed someone to show them how to walk in it. So in 1976, with two staff members and three volunteers, Colson founded Prison Fellowship Ministries as an interdenominational ministry to prisoners, ex-prisoners, and their families.

Today, PF is an international movement of God's people

fueling the crime-related ministry of the local church around the world. In the United States alone, the organization mobilizes some 50,000 volunteers who teach and model the love of God to those who so desperately need to know him.

PF's most popular program is Angel Tree®, through which church volunteers provide prisoners' children with Christmas gifts, presented on behalf of the imprisoned parent and in the name of Jesus. PF encourages prisoners to provide information, so volunteers can contact the families directly. Volunteers also deliver gospel materials donated by the American Bible Society. Many churches have caught the vision for follow-up ministry to prisoners' families—inviting them into regular church programs and sponsoring special programs, such as Bible studies, field trips, and summer camps.

Volunteers work with prisoners in a number of settings. Traditionally, PF's feature program has been the In-Prison Seminar, which is three days of biblically based teaching reinforced by small-group discussions led by volunteers. Skits, object lessons, songs, and visual aids work together to focus the inmates' attention on the gospel message.

Weekly Bible studies pick up where an In-Prison Seminar leaves off. Bible study guidebooks, published by PF in English and Spanish, draw participants deeper into seminar topics such as *Growing in Christ* and *Loving Others*. While PF Bible studies stress the spiritual basics of Bible reading, prayer, and service to others, trained volunteers are also sensitive to the particular spiritual needs of the individual inmates before them, "changing channels" if necessary to address specific concerns.

Most hardened prisoners do not rush to see "what's happening" at a weekly Bible study or optional seminar. But PF has learned they will show up for an afternoon of lively entertainment that includes a hard-hitting gospel presentation. Every year PF targets specific states, working with prison officials and church leaders to organize intense, areawide Starting Line evangelistic campaigns that feature testimonies of high-profile Christian athletes or entertainers and rely on many local volunteers for the event and follow-up.

In 1997, PF embarked on a revolutionary partnership with the Texas Department of Criminal Justice. In one minimum-security prison near Houston, for up to two hundred voluntary participants near release, PF has taken charge of all round-the-clock programming, drawing heavily on volunteers from local churches. For eighteen months, prisoners are immersed in a Christian environment—worship, education, work skills, personal accountability. They're matched with mentors who stay with them when they're released. PF looks forward to expanding this program in other states.

Many PF volunteers faithfully minister to inmates without ever stepping inside prison gates. As pen pals, their letters from the outside can brighten even the darkest of prison days. One volunteer who writes to six prisoners says, "Five accepted Jesus after being in prison. And one has recently asked me to pray for his salvation. Each one has become a special friend."

Working with ex-prisoners nationwide, PF's new program, A Network for Life® (NFL), functions through local licensed "service groups." They're weekly support groups—but more.

Veteran ex-prisoners and other volunteers mentor newcomers in transition. And community service is a vital "outward" focus.

Prison Fellowship Ministries has two vital subsidiaries, one being Neighbors Who Care®, dedicated to minister to crime victims. Church-based volunteers in select cities reach out to victims of violent and property crimes, providing crime-scene cleanup, help with document replacement, emergency food or funds, emotional support, prayer, and spiritual aid.

In addition, Justice Fellowship® (JF), an affiliate ministry founded in 1983, strives to conform America's criminal justice system to biblical standards of justice. Restorative Justice, as JF calls it, demands that offenders be held accountable for their crimes, that broken relationships be restored, that restitution be made to victims, and that the community be involved and protected. JF is also at the forefront of efforts to protect religious freedom for prisoners and all Americans.

Prison Fellowship Ministries in the United States is just one of eighty-three chartered PF ministries in the Prison Fellowship International (PFI) association. Each national ministry addresses crime-related ministry needs unique to its own locale.

PFI organizes a Global Assistance Programme, through which volunteer teams travel overseas to assist in the construction of buildings and provide medical and dental care and business consultation to prisoners, ex-prisoners, and their families.

Around the world, Prison Fellowship affords Christians opportunities to live out their faith with love, creativity, and compassion. If you have finished this book prayerfully wondering, "Well, what can *I* do?" God will be faithful to reveal whatever particular ministry he would have you pursue. And if you would like to know more about Prison Fellowship and the opportunities it offers, please write to Prison Fellowship, P.O. Box 17500, Washington, D.C., 20041-0500.

For more information, including addresses of local Prison Fellowship offices, check out the following Prison Fellowship websites:

www.prisonfellowship.org

www.breakpoint.org

www.angeltree.org

www.justicefellowship.org

www.neighborswhocare.org


### Tune in to "Breakpoint"

On 425 stations nationwide, Chuck Colson gives a five-minute weekday radio commentary. These hard-hitting "Breakpoint" commentaries challenge the church to live out a reasoned and proactive faith, equipping believers to contend for the truth and lovingly challenge the "barbarism" of the day. Station information and commentary transcripts are available at www.breakpoint.org.

# N O T E S

## Chapter 1—Intimations of Decline

1. Dan Oldenburg, "Kids and Morals in a Me-First World," *Washington Post* (March 25, 1988): D5.
2. Malcolm Muggeridge, *Vintage Muggeridge* (Grand Rapids: Eerdmans Publishing Company, 1985), 104.

## Chapter 2—The Barbarian Invasion: Tracing the Roots

1. Eric Voegelin, *From Enlightenment to Revolution*, ed. John H. Hallowell (Durham, N.C.: Duke University Press, 1975), 85.
2. Ibid., 81.
3. John Stuart Mill, *On Liberty* (Indianapolis: Hackett Publishing Company, 1978), 12.
4. Ibid., 64.
5. Richard Weaver, *Ideas Have Consequences* (Chicago: University of Chicago Press, 1948), 80.

## Chapter 3—Islands in the Stream

1. Alexis de Tocqueville, *Democracy in America*, trans. George Lawrence (New York: Anchor Books, 1969), 2:508.
2. James Hitchcock, *What Is Secular Humanism?* (Ann Arbor: Servant Books, 1982), 66.
3. Samuel Beckett, *Waiting for Godot* (New York: Grove Press, 1954), 59.
4. Ibid., back cover.
5. Quoted in Malcolm Muggeridge, *A Third Testament* (Boston: Little, Brown and Company, 1976), 129.

## Chapter 4—The Reign of Relativism

1. Carl F.H. Henry, *Twilight of a Great Civilization* (Westchester, Ill.: Crossway Books, 1988), 170.
2. Justice Brennan, writing for the five-member majority, labeled the expressed secular purpose of the legislation—academic balance—a "sham." But he, like Brokaw, cited no evidence other than that these were religious people who had sponsored the amendment.
3. C.S. Lewis, *The Screwtape Letters* (New York: Macmillan, 1961), x.
4. Alasdair MacIntyre, *After Virtue* (Notre Dame: Notre Dame Press, 1981), 236.
5. Walker Percy, *The Thanatos Syndrome* (New York: Farrar, Straus, and Giroux, 1987), 127-28.

## Chapter 5—Decadence and Decline

1. Russell Kirk, *Confessions of a Bohemian Tory* (New York: Fleet Publishing Corporation, 1963), 222.
2. Henry Fairlie, *The Seven Deadly Sins Today* (Washington, D.C.: New Republic Books, 1978), 118, 120.

## Chapter 6—Men without Chests

1. Oldenburg, "Kids and Morals."
2. Ibid.
3. "The Culture of Apathy," *The New Republic* (February 8, 1988):7.
4. Quoted in *The Wit and Wisdom of the 20th Century*, ed. Frank S. Pepper (New York: Peter Bedrick Books, 1987), 74.
5. Quoted in Russell Kirk, *Beyond the Dreams of Avarice* (Chicago: Henry Regnery Company, 1956), 159.
6. C.S. Lewis, *The Abolition of Man* (New York: Macmillan, 1947), 34.
7. Fairlie, *Seven Deadly Sins*, 129.

## Chapter 7—Barbarians in the Parlor

1. "Too Young to Die," *Christianity Today* (March 20, 1987):19.
2. Fairlie, *Seven Deadly Sins*, 118.
3. Judith Martin, *Miss Manners' Guide to Excruciatingly Correct Behavior* (New York: Warner Books, 1982), 49.

## Chapter 8—Barbarians in the Classroom

1. Barbara Walters television special, "America's Kids: Why They Flunk," October, 1988.
2. Allan Bloom, *The Closing of the American Mind* (New York: Simon and Schuster, 1987), 25-26.
3. Midge Decter, "Sex Education on Trial," *Crisis* (December, 1988):40-43.
4. Derek Bok, "Ethics, the University and Society," *Harvard Magazine* (May-June, 1988):40.
5. Ibid.
6. Allan Bloom quoted in Robert L. Spaeth, "Individualism vs. the Liberal Arts," *Current* (March-April, 1988):9.
7. Bok, "Ethics," 39.
8. Gregory Wolf quoted in James V. Schall, "On the Platonic Lie," *Crisis* (February, 1988):42.
9. Bloom, *Closing*, 26.
10. Spaeth, "Individualism vs. Liberal."
11. Ibid., 10.

## Chapter 9—Barbarians in Power

1. Mary Coleridge, *Poems* (1908), cxxi.
2. As reported in *World Press Review* (February, 1988):13.
3. After public criticism, Senator Inouye withdrew the proposal.
4. Judges 17:6.
5. Fairlie, *Seven Deadly Sins*, 114.
6. Hendrick Smith, *The Power Game* (New York: Random House, 1988), 26.
7. Arthur Schlesinger quoted in Richard Neuhaus, *Naked Public Square* (Grand Rapids: Eerdmans Publishing Company, 1984), 91.
8. Peter L. Berger, "Religion in Post-Protestant America," *Commentary* 81:5 (May, 1986):44.

## Chapter 10—Barbarians in the Pews

1. Robert Bellah, *Habits of the Heart* (Berkeley: University of California Press, 1985), 228.
2. Ibid., 221.
3. *Georgetown's Blue and Grey* (Spring 1988):22.
4. Ibid., 1.
5. Besides, Georgetown's president wrote in a foggy ten-page

letter to alumni, "The University's presence in this delicate area of teaching is needed, but may well also appeal to those to whom it is directed both as an interference and a disputable one at that." (Heaven forbid that the church call sin "sin" and thus "interfere" with anyone's free choice.)

Maybe Georgetown just suffered from legal exhaustion; after all, the school fought the case for eight years. But it is hard to avoid the suspicion that the school caved in to the pressure of "enlightened" opinion. No institution, particularly one as prominent as Georgetown, wants to risk being seen by the Washington community as a bastion of homophobia.

One thing is clear, however. Georgetown's refusal to contest the court's decision has allowed this intrusive legislation to stand, spelling danger to other religious institutions in the nation's capitol. Landmark court decisions of this type provide a precedent, a model of sorts. Though not directly binding elsewhere, they are often used to support legal arguments in similar cases.

6. William F. Fore, *Television and Religion* (Minneapolis: Augsburg Publishing House, 1987), 89.
7. All the John Shelby Spong quotations are from "Sex and Sin," *Washington Post* (Sunday, July 31, 1988): C4.
8. Clayton Carlson, head of Harper and Row's religious publishing division, quoted in *Publisher's Weekly* (November 18, 1988).

## Chapter 11—The Great Nightfall?

1. Robert Bellah, *Habits of the Heart*, 285.
2. Russell Kirk, *The Roots of American Order* (LaSalle, Ill.: Open Court, 1974), 84.
3. T.S. Eliot, *Christianity and Culture* (New York: Harcourt Brace Jovanovich, Inc., 1968), 18.
4. G.K. Chesterton, *A Chesterton Anthology*, ed. P.J. Kavanagh (San Francisco: Ignatius Press, 1985), 359.
5. Quoted in Russell Kirk, "The Wise Men Know What Wicked Things Are Written on the Sky," *Modern Age* (Spring, 1985):113.
6. Surely there is a precedent for this. For as Rome died, Christianity grew up strong out of its very decay.
7. Quoted in Kirk, "Wise Men."
8. Esther 4:14, *New International Version*.
9. Ibid., 4:16.

## Chapter 12—God and Politics

1. Kirk, "Wise Men," 113.
2. *Wall Street Journal* (May 31, 1988).

## Chapter 13—Moral Education

1. Matthew Arnold quoted in James M. Houston, *I Believe in the Creator* (Grand Rapids: Eerdman's Publishing Company, 1980), 175.
2. Quoted in Kirk, "Wise Men," 69.
3. Kirk, *Dreams of Avarice*, 155.
4. Quoted in Kirk, "Wise Men," 24.
5. Ibid., 55.

## Chapter 14—Paradox

1. From a speech at Congress on the Bible, September 1987.
2. Quoted in Russell Hittinger, "The Two Cities and the Modern World: A Dawsonian Assessment," *Modern Age* (Spring/Summer, 1984): 193.

## Chapter 15—Metanoia

1. Neuhaus, Congress on the Bible.
2. All of Gordon Liddy's quotes in this section are taken from the transcript of a speech he delivered at a Good Friday prayer breakfast, April 17, 1988.

## Chapter 16—The Wild Truth

1. E.B. White, *One Man's Meat* (New York: Harper Colophon, 1982), 135.
2. Quoted in James Boice, *Does Inerrancy Matter?* (ICBF Foundation Series).
3. Ibid.
4. "Divino Afflante Spiritu," September 30, 1943, from *The Papal*

*Encyclicals 1939-1958* (McGrath Publishing Company, 1981).
5. From a speech by Paul Johnson entitled "An Historian Looks at Jesus."
6. Ibid.
7. Chesterton, *Anthology,* 297.

## Chapter 17—Communities of Light

1. Exodus 29:45.
2. 1 Peter 2:9.
3. Hittinger, "The Two Cities," 197.
4. Armando Valladares, *Against All Hope* (New York: Ballantine Books, 1986), 421.

## Chapter 18—The Christian Mind

1. Harry Blamires, *The Christian Mind* (Ann Arbor: Servant Books, 1978), 3-4.

## Chapter 19—The Moral Imagination

1. Peter Berger, *The Capitalist Revolution: Fifty Propositions About Prosperity, Equality, and Liberty* (New York: Basic Books, Inc., 1986), 195.
2. Kirk, "Wise Men," 113-14.
3. Russell Kirk, *Enemies of the Permanent Things,* 119.
4. William Manchester, *The Last Lion: Visions of Glory* (New York: Dell Publishing Company, 1985), 4.
5. William Manchester, *The Last Lion: Alone* (Boston: Little, Brown and Company, 1988), 686.
6. Ibid., 687.
7. Bellah, *Habits of the Heart,* 295.
8. Even as we identify ourselves as resolutely pro-life, we must understand that the way Christians define their terms can make all the difference in one's focus and agenda. It is important that we explore and understand these distinctions.

   Cardinal Joseph Bernardin of Chicago has attacked those who call themselves pro-life but who don't support a "consistent ethic of life," which would include issues like racial tension, homelessness, government economic policies, and, above all, nuclear deterrence.

Bernardin has labeled his argument "the seamless garment"—the idea that to be consistently pro-life one must oppose both abortion *and* nuclear deterrence, euthanasia *and* the economic exploitation inherent to industrial capitalism—anything that its proponents believe threatens human life and dignity.

The effect of radical applications of the seamless garment argument, however, is to transform *respect* for life into *veneration* of life. Biological life becomes the overriding human value. Anything that threatens it must be resisted.

The question then naturally arises: What price are we prepared to pay to preserve biological life? If we are willing to protect life at *any* cost, then the price we pay will be too high.

Some things, such as justice and freedom, must be more important than life if life is to be worth anything at all. If we lack the moral resolve to die, and even to kill, to preserve these principles against those who assault them, then we will end up both betraying our principles *and* losing our lives.

The distinction between respect for life and veneration of life is as wide as the chasm between civilization and barbarism. Paradoxically, venerating life is life negating, not life affirming. It holds every other human value hostage, and then, one by one, executes them.

9. Quoted in Joseph Sobran, "Pensees: Notes for the Reactionary of Tomorrow," *National Review* (December 31, 1985):50.

10. Kirk, "Wise Men," 117.

## Chapter 20—Against the Night

1. From "The Ballad of the White Horse," *The Collected Poems of G.K. Chesterton* (New York: Dodd, Mead and Company, 1980), 216-217.

# INDEX

# STUDY GUIDE

## STUDY 1
### Decay and Change
*The times smell of sunset.*

**Read**

*Against the Night*, Prologue and chapter 1
Psalm 90
Isaiah 5:20-21
Ecclesiastes 3

**Reflect**

1. Some changes are part of the natural order of things and are inevitable. What changes in your life fall into this category?
2. Other changes can be reversed. Give examples from your own life.
3. What do you think the author means by the phrase "new barbarians"? Look up the word "barbarian" if necessary.

**Apply**

Could you in any way be mistaken for a "new barbarian"? If so, what would you change about yourself?

**Pray**

Pray for our society, using the prayer in Psalm 90 as a starting point. Pray that God might show you what you can do.

# STUDY 2
## Individualism

*"I am different from all men I have seen. If I am not better, at least I am different."*

—Jean Jacques Rousseau

**Read**

*Against the Night,* chapters 2 and 3

Mark 8:34-37

1 Corinthians 13:4-7

John 8:31-32

Romans 12:3

**Reflect**

1. What evidences of individualism do you see in your community?

2. We've all been influenced by individualism to some extent. What factors make it difficult at times for you to make and sustain commitments?

3. How has individualism affected your church? your family? yourself?

**Apply**

How will you deal with those aspects of your own life that have been overtaken by individualism?

**Pray**

Pray that God will help you resist the influence of individualism and enable you to make and keep significant commitments to others.

# STUDY 3
## Relativism

*For if self is the locus of truth, what more moral quest could there be than to find oneself? There is no universal truth, no absolute code of conduct; there is only truth for me and truth for you.*

**Read**

*Against the Night,* chapter 4
2 Corinthians 10:3-5
Hosea 4:6
Isaiah 59:14

**Reflect**

1. Beliefs as firm as bedrock since early Christianity have been eroded by relativism. Which eroded beliefs are most obvious? Which ones are most subtle?

2. As a Christian, what values do you find hard to talk about with unbelievers? At what point does the discussion become difficult? Why? Is it ever because you yourself are unclear about your values or are affected by relativistic tendencies?

3. Which values might you be tempted to compromise at

work or in the community, or even in your home?

4. How can we discern what's right among the competing values in our culture? How can we know which claims of authority to trust?

**Apply**

Can you identify places in your life eroded by relativism, even relativistic choices you have made? How will you strengthen those areas?

**Pray**

Pray that God will help you clearly discern his truth in this day of shifting values. Pray that you will become aware of specific instances in your life where you may be tempted to compromise your values due to relativism.

# STUDY 4
## Loss of Character

*"Men and women become decadent when they forget or deny the objects of life, and so fritter away their years in trifles or debauchery."*

—Russell Kirk

**Read**

*Against the Night*, chapters 5 and 6
Romans 1:18-38
Romans 5:3-5
Colossians 3:12-17
Romans 12:2

**Reflect**

1. Examples of loss of character abound. Consider some examples, both in the public forum and lesser known situations from your personal sphere.

2. What makes it so hard to break bad habits and establish good ones? What does it take to reverse the direction of character in someone's life?

3. How has the church been affected by the loss of character in our culture?

**Apply**

How can you guard your own character and help others guard theirs?

**Pray**

Pray that God will help you grow in character and encourage others in the same direction. Pray that the direction of culture will be reversed.

# STUDY 5
## The Family

*"Haven't you read ... that at the beginning the Creator 'made them male and female,' and said, 'For this reason a man will leave his father and mother and be united to his wife, and the two will become one flesh'? So they are no longer two, but one. Therefore what God has joined together, let man not separate."*

MATTHEW 19:4-6, NIV

**Read**
*Against the Night*, chapter 7
Matthew 19:1-12
Ephesians 5:22–6:4
Colossians 3:18-21

**Reflect**
1. Scarcely any family remains untouched by divorce. Keeping in mind the lack of moral influence in most marriages, give some central reasons for the divorces you have observed.
2. What responsibility do we have to confront friends' noticeable marital problems before it's too late?
3. What are the difficulties in being a single parent? How can friends give support?
4. If parents don't "civilize" their children, who does? What are the dangers of leaving childhood training to amoral or immoral characters?

**Apply**
How can you better model moral virtue, strengthening not just your own family but those who look to you?

**Pray**
Pray that God will help you be faithful in your family situation. Pray that there might be a widespread recovery of family values in our nation. Pray for specific individuals whom you feel are in the forefront of the battle for the family.

# STUDY 6
## Education

*"If you ask what is the good of education, the answer is easy—that education makes good men, and that good men act nobly."*

—Plato

### Read
*Against the Night*, chapter 8
Proverbs 9:8-9; 15:31; 21:11; 22:6

### Reflect
1. Tolerance and openness are often proclaimed as being of ultimate importance. Name some good and bad kinds of tolerance and openness.
2. We need to maintain tolerance, in its good sense, in several forms: legal, social, intellectual. How can we have tolerance without letting it slip into relativism?
3. Can you think of examples of good and bad kinds of closedness?
4. Propose some solutions to our educational problems.

### Apply
What can you do to make sure any students within your influence are headed in the direction of truth?

### Pray
Pray that you may be open to God's truth and open to reproof, especially from godly people. Pray for God's wisdom. Pray that you might be made aware of any way you may be tempted to compromise God's truth.

# STUDY 7
## Politics

*American politics simply mirrors the loss of character in the American people. If citizens are not willing to put the civic good above their own, they can't expect their leaders to do it for them.*

### Read
*Against the Night,* chapter 9
Romans 13:1-7
2 Chronicles 7:14

### Reflect
1. Why does "separation of church and state" not mean the separation of the state from God? What role should faith play in the making of laws?
2. Reflect on the difference between traditional pluralism (see p. 92) and the "new pluralism" (p. 93). Suggest some ways we could return from the "new pluralism" (with its lack of transcendent standards) to the old.
3. What can we expect government to do for society? Are there things government should not do that it now does?
4. Some say politics should never be based on self-interest. Do you agree? Substantiate your answer.

### Apply
How have you, perhaps through economic interests or causes you support, contributed to the condition of our government? How can you use your influence to help your legislators restore transcendent values to the lawmaking process?

**Pray**

Pray that we might humble ourselves, seek God's face, and repent of our sins. God will hear from heaven and forgive our sin and heal our land.

# STUDY 8
## The Church
*"Religion up, morality down."*

—George Gallup

**Read**

*Against the Night,* chapters 10 and 11

1 Peter 2:9-10

Matthew 16:18

Revelation 3:14-22

**Reflect**

1. Few churches stand untouched by moral decline. Where have compromises been made? How have churches around you been affected?
2. The church contributes to individualism and relativism, many times without intention. Name some ways.
3. Why is it vital that the church maintain its distinctiveness from culture? Is it possible for the church to use elements of culture to attract unbelievers without losing its distinctiveness?

**Apply**

How will you, as a member of the church, the "royal priesthood," seek to serve the Lord without compromise?

**Pray**

Pray that the Lord might give you a vision for what you can do in your church. Pray that he might help you to make a difference in dealing with the loss of character in our congregations.

## STUDY 9
### Moral Education

*"There is little hope for democracy if the hearts of men and women in democratic societies cannot be touched by a call to something greater than ourselves."*

—Margaret Thatcher

**Read**

*Against the Night,* chapters 12 and 13
Titus 1:15-16
1 Timothy 4:1-2
Acts 24:16
Jeremiah 31:33-34

**Reflect**

1. Reflect on where you received your moral education. What do you see that bears out Robert Bellah's statement on "communities of memory"? How can moral education avoid becoming legalistic?

2. What, specifically, should the church do to encourage moral education at home and in church settings? How can parents carry out the task of educating their children's consciences?

3. How do we correct our consciences when they are in error? How do we tell if they're in error?

4. Why is it we so often know something to be true—yet refuse to act on it?

## Apply

How will you contribute to the moral education of the next generation?

## Pray

Pray that you might grow in the knowledge and wisdom of God. Pray that you might make a difference in your family or church in encouraging moral education.

# STUDY 10
## The Church and Repentance

*The repentance God desires is not just contrition over particular sins; it is also a daily attitude, a perspective.*

## Read

*Against the Night,* chapters 14 and 15
Psalm 51
2 Corinthians 7:10

## Reflect

1. Why is it so difficult for us to admit our sin?

2. Why does the renewal of our individual lives or of the church require repentance?

3. Name some attributes of God that, if we pause to consider them, will cause and encourage repentance.

4. What impact could a repentant church have? Why?

## Apply

Is yours a life of repentance? What changes in your life-style must you make to maintain a pure, repentant heart?

What is the most significant lesson you learned from this study?

## Pray

Ask God to reveal to you any sins of which you have been unaware. Pray Psalm 51 as a prayer of contrition.

# STUDY 11
## Truth and Light

*Orthodoxy often requires us to be hard precisely where the world is soft, and soft where the world is hard.*

## Read

*Against the Night*, chapters 16 and 17

John 14:6

Matthew 5:14-16

## Reflect

1. Why do you think Christ is the Truth?

2. What are the best reasons you know to believe that the Scriptures are true and reliable?

3. We never know until we're there, but how prepared do you feel to be God's representative of truth and light in a situation of total darkness?

## Apply

How will you make sure you are walking with a sure step on the path of truth?

## Pray

Pray that you might more clearly know what you believe and why you believe it. Pray that you might be light in a dark world.

# STUDY 12
## Moral Imagination

*If Christianity is true, then it cannot be simply a file drawer in our crowded lives. It must be the central truth from which all our behavior, relationships, and philosophy flow.*

## Read

*Against the Night*, chapters 18 and 19
John 8:31-32
Deuteronomy 6:4-8

## Reflect

1. Have you seen in your own life a tendency to compartmentalize your Christianity? How can you better allow your faith to permeate all of your life and not just the "religious" parts?

2. How can one appeal to the imagination without sacrificing truth?

3. Why should we pursue what Harry Blamires calls a "Christian mind"? (See Matthew 22:37 for a start.)

4. What will the development of a "Christian mind" involve for you and your church?

**Apply**

How will you change your reading habits and whatever else so that you not merely grow in self-improvement or self-analysis or self-indulgence but can help transform our culture by making the Christian worldview appealing to those within your influence?

**Pray**

Pray that you will gain the wisdom and discernment to "think Christianly" in every part of your life and schedule. Pray that you would discern fresh ways to communicate truth to your skeptical friends and neighbors.

# STUDY 13
## Against the Night

*"But the men signed of the cross of Christ*
*Go gaily in the dark."*

—G.K. Chesterton

**Read**

*Against the Night*, chapter 20, and review past studies
Psalm 85

Habakkuk 3:17-19
Matthew 7:24-27

**Reflect**
1. What difference can you as an individual make?
2. What difference can your church or study group make?
3. What are some further books that you want to read? other steps you would like to take to allow God to strengthen you against the night?
4. How have your prayers changed over the course of reading this book?

**Apply**
Will your life really look or be any different as a result of this study? What are some long-range plans you can make to stay on the track of preparedness and zeal?

**Pray**
Pray that God will revive the church and the nation. Use Psalm 85 as the framework for your prayers.